THE MOON VEILS VULCAN
AND
THE SUN VEILS NEPTUNE

by
Kurt Abraham

LAMPUS PRESS
P.O. Box 463
Jacksonville, Oregon 97530

First published in 1989 by
Lampus Press
Jacksonville, OR

ISBN 0-9609002-4-1
Library of Congress Catalogue Card Number: 89-84278

Printed in the United States of America

BOOKS BY KURT ABRAHAM

Introduction to the Seven Rays

Psychological Types and the Seven Rays, Vol. I

Threefold Method for Understanding the Seven Rays and Other Essays in Esoteric Psychology

The Seven Rays and Nations: France and the United States Compared

The Moon Veils Vulcan and the Sun Veils Neptune

CREDITS

For permission to use copyright material the author gratefully acknowledges the following:

The Lucis Trust for permission to quote from Alice Bailey's *Esoteric Astrology, Treatise on White Magic, Treatise on Cosmic Fire, Discipleship in the New Age, vol. I, Esoteric Healing, Rays and Initiations,* and *Glamour: A World Problem.*

The Agni Yoga Society (319 West 107th Street, New York, NY 10025) for permission to quote from *Heart.*

Philosophical Library Publishers for permission to quote from *The Diary of Soren Kierkegaard.*

CONTENTS

The Moon Veils Vulcan

In *Esoteric Astrology* D. K. mentions that "the moon is spoken of in the ancient teaching as 'veiling either Vulcan or Uranus.'" He suggests that astrologers "work with Vulcan when dealing with the undeveloped or average man and with Uranus when considering the highly developed man" (Bailey, 1951, p. 13). Later in the same book, D. K. gives three planets "which the Moon may be veiling . . . Vulcan, Neptune or Uranus" (p. 219).

There are several factors to be considered here: (1) What is the influence of the moon, generally speaking, viewed from the esoteric angle? (2) What is the Vulcan influence or energy? (3) What is meant by the term "veiling"? (4) Are there levels of development or evolutionary stages implied by the veiling of *three* planets? (5) How can these factors be characterized so that we move the abstract concept to vital understanding and practical application?

A more fundamental question still: Does such a planet, given the name of Vulcan, actually exist? In this regard, D. K. mentions that "Vulcan is one of the veiled and hidden planets and one which is, therefore, little known or understood" (Bailey, 1951, p. 392). In the essay on hidden planets we look into some of the hints D. K. has given on this most difficult and mysterious subject. "The Ageless Wisdom claims that there are around seventy 'hidden' planets in our solar system" (Bailey, 1951, p. 6). It is highly probable that "hidden" refers to non-physical, i.e., etheric, astral, and mental planets or planetary influences . . . but more on this later. Suffice it to say at this point that as humanity and as groups within the human family develop, they become sensitive to subtler planetary and astrological influences. Evidently, the human condition has reached a point where one such esoteric influence, namely Vulcan (among others), is now becoming a "real" factor or a factor of relationship vis-à-vis the Earth. Our effort here is to find out whether or not we can in fact determine such psychological energies affecting humanity, and, if we can, then how can we work with them in an intelligent manner?

The Moon's Influence. From an esoteric point of view, we are told that the Moon is "nothing more than a dead form" and that it has "no emanation and no radiation . . . no quality of her own." Yet the Moon does have an effect, which is noted as a "thought effect . . . as a result of a powerful and most ancient thoughtform" (Bailey, 1951, p. 13).

The apparent contradiction that the Moon is a dead form yet still has an effect is further clarified in the following passage from *Esoteric Healing:* "The moon, as you know, is a shell, an ancient form through which the planetary Logos at one time sought expression. It is slowly disintegrating physically but not astrally as yet, and is therefore still closely linked with the astral body of the planetary Logos and therefore with the astral bodies of all people" (Bailey, 1953, p. 341). In *White Magic* we find that "in the moon influence, we have indicated the native's *past*. It summarizes the limitations and handicaps under which he must work, and therefore might be regarded as embodying the tamasic aspect of matter, or that which 'holds back' and which—if permitted to influence unduly—will produce inertia. In the body with which man is equipped lies hid the secret of past experience, and every lunar form through which we have to arrive at due expression is in itself the product or synthesis of all the past. . . . The influence of the moon is primarily physical. The prison of the soul is thus indicated. The handicaps to be met are thus secured; the type of body or bodies through which the force of the native's sign and the quality of the energy which will bring him to his goal are thus defined. Through the medium of the lunar lords and what they have given him as the result of past experience down the ages must he express himself upon the physical plane" (Bailey, 1934, pp. 435, 436).

In summary, the Moon:

—has an astral or emotional influence
—has a tamasic influence, a tendency to produce inertia

—defines (and thus limits and handicaps) the bodies or vehicles of expression (thus also a physical influence)
—the limiting influence is a result of past experience

If the Moon is the tamasic or inertia aspect, then the Sun, as it represents personality, is the rajasic or activity aspect, and the rising sign, indicating direction towards the soul, is the sattvic or rhythm aspect, producing "harmony with the will of the soul" (Bailey, 1934, p. 435).

In *Treatise on Cosmic Fire* it is mentioned that every Moon is a "point of corruption, or that which is passing off in noxious gases. The transmutation of the form has been proceeded with in their case to a point where all that represents *vital* energy has left, all solar life has passed off, no remnants of pranic energy remain, and that which is to be seen is simply the decay of the physical body,—a decay which is proceeding on etheric levels as well as on physical. The decay of the moon has as great an evil effect upon all that contacts it as a decaying body on earth has upon its surroundings. It is occultly 'offensive.' This will be more truly apprehended when the etheric double of our moon is studied. As the moon becomes small through the process of disintegration, its effect upon the Earth will be correspondingly lessened, and this stage will be paralleled by a consequent greater freedom from evil impulse of the sons of men. Better conditions among the animals will be another result above all else, and the dying out of that which is noxious in the animal kingdom" (Bailey, 1925, pp. 794–5). We are also told that "the Moon brings about the inclination to create these conditions which lead to the great and critical transformations of instinct into intellect" (Bailey, 1951, p. 139).

Identifying some of the polarities might help us understand the Moon influence:

Moon	Sun
past	present
limitation, decay	development, growth
inertia	activity
instinct	intellect

In the triplicity Form-Soul-Spirit or Matter-Consciousness-Life, the Moon is related to the Form-Matter aspect. The function of the form on the positive side is to protect, to nurture, to provide experience, to grow through activity, etc. Negatively, when there is attachment to form beyond its particular cyclic use, form becomes an impediment or obstruction. In other words, when the form has served its purpose, it ought to be relinquished, shed, rejected, sacrificed—it ought to die. The form aspect at one level is the dense physical form. From another angle, that is from the angle of soul, the three worlds of personality expression (physical, emotional, lower mental) are all part of the form aspect. Instinct guides the form in that instinct is an automatic, unthinking, mechanical process that protects and nurtures the pre-self-conscious form unit. As the capacity for thought is introduced (lower mind, intellect), then which way will it go? How will it be directioned? Will thought feed instinctual attachments until they become something else, causing form to live beyond its time and in a distorted, *unplanned* fashion? Or will thought make its higher connection with the true Thinker, the Soul?

The Moon represents in a sense where we have already been. It is attractive and alluring and seductive. It is deeply subconscious. It is what we inexplicably feel in the loins and the gut, rather than what we subtly sense in the heart and in the top of the head. It is inertia and reluctance to move on. It is the resting and the suffering of an imprisoning attitude in order to avoid coming face to face with the limitations of ourselves. The subtlest form is a mental form, and the subtlest mental form that is an obstruction, rather than a vessel or vehicle of manifestation, is a "veil."

When the soul builds and controls the outer form, there is health and the manifestation of a constructive force. "The results are wholeness, right relationship and correct activity. . . . When the soul is not in control, and the forces of the form nature are therefore the controlling factors, there will be ill health. The builders of the form are the 'lunar lords', the physical, astral and mental elementals. These in their triple totality compose the personality. They are occultly under the direction of the moon, the symbol of form, called often the 'mother of the form' " (Bailey, 1953, p. 608).

In the *Secret Doctrine* we find a confirming statement that the influences of the Moon are "psychophysiological." The Moon is analogous to a corpse, "sending out injurious emanations" and "vampirizing the earth and its inhabitants." "Esoterically, the moon is the symbol of the Lower Manas; it is also the symbol of the Astral" (Vol. 5, p. 535).

The question then becomes: What is the way? How to deal with the negative influence? How can we escape from the "noxious gases"? How can we free ourselves from the limitations of the past, our own past, the limitations that we ourselves have created? How can we break free from the handicaps of our physical, astral and mental (lower manas) bodies? How to work free from the tremendous weight of inertia?

The Moon Veils Vulcan. In esoteric astrology and in esoteric psychology a key dynamic deals with *energy substitution*. An energy that leads towards growth (the next step ahead) is substituted for the energy or force that is responsible for a static, confining condition. "The moment that a man becomes aware of his own soul and is endeavoring to control his own 'path in life,' the influence of the planets, per se, definitely weakens and steadily become less and less; his personality chart appears inconclusive and often most inaccurate. It is the force flowing *through* the planets and not the force *of* the planets themselves which then governs and controls. The man then becomes receptive to the subtler and higher energies of the solar system and of the twelve governing constellations" (Bailey, 1951, p. 16). What we are evidently looking for here is a substitution of a subtler energy of the solar system (Vulcan) for the limitations and inertia of the past (Moon). I believe it would be accurate to say that for the vast majority of mankind, the "Moon veils Vulcan." The state of consciousness known as "the Moon" provides tremendous resistance to meaningful change. Resting on the past is a desire for and a regression to an unconscious, unthinking state. "Veil" is an appropriate metaphor in that it is a thin film-like substance that distorts perception. One can see through a veil but in an unclear, partial way. One has the illusion of seeing, the illusion of knowing. Only when the veil is lifted do we see how distorted our perception was. In order to break through the veil it seems that among other things Vulcan indicates an intense labor and a first ray energy. There is then a sensed higher purpose and a willingness to make personal sacrifice in order to be a self-effacing and minuscule part in a grand and timeless work.

Vulcan. More specifically, what can be said about the energy of Vulcan? "At the first initiation, the disciple has to contend with the crystallizing and destroying forces of Vulcan and Pluto" (Bailey, 1951, p. 70).

"Man comes, therefore, through the Moon—under bondage of form in order through form experience to achieve release and the uplift of matter in Vulcan" (p. 127).

"The Moon or Vulcan stands for the glorification, through purification and detachment, of matter" (p. 216).

"Vulcan brings in what might be called the endurance aspect of the will-to-be. . . . This necessitates persistence, endurance and continuity of effort and is one of the characteristics imparted or stimulated by energies pouring from Vulcan" (p. 274).

"Vulcan is governed by the first ray, and the first ray and the first kingdom [mineral] are definitely bound together" (p. 386).

To summarize:

Vulcan
—first ray of will and power
—persistence, endurance, the will-to-be
—affects physical plane, mineral kingdom
—glorification of matter (form) through detachment and
  purification
—uplift and release from bondage of form (Moon)

Are we any closer at this point to identifying the Vulcan energy? In Greek mythology Hephaestus (Vulcan) was the lame Smith-god, dropped from the height of Olympus by his mother Hera (Earth), who was embarrassed by his pitiful appearance. "He survived this misadventure, however, without bodily damage, because he fell into the sea, where Thetis and Eurynome were at hand to rescue him. These gentle goddesses kept him with them in an underwater grotto, where he set up his first smithy and rewarded their kindness by making them all sorts of ornamental and useful objects. One day, when nine years had passed, Hera met Thetis, who happened to be wearing a brooch of his workmanship and asked: 'My dear, where in the world did you find that wonderful jewel? Thetis hesitated before replying, but Hera forced the truth from her. At once she fetched Hephaestus back to Olympus, where she set him up in a much finer smithy, with twenty bellows working day and night, made much of him, and arranged that he should marry Aphrodite [Venus]. Hephaestus became so far reconciled with Hera that he dared reproach Zeus himself for hanging her by the wrists from Heaven when she rebelled against him. But silence would have been wiser, because angry Zeus only heaved him down from Olympus a second time. He was a whole day falling. On striking the earth of the island of Lemnos, he broke both legs and, though immortal, had little left in his body when the islanders found him" (Robert Graves, 1955, pp. 86–87).

According to Graves, both Eurynome and Thetis are associated with the moon: "Eurynome was the goddess's title [the Goddess of All Things or universal goddess] as the visible moon" (Graves, 1955, p. 28). "Thetis, Amphitrite, and Nereis were different local titles of the Triple Moon-goddess as ruler of the sea" (p. 61). It seems interesting that in the symbolism of the myth we find Hephaestus (Vulcan) working in the depths (below the surface of the ocean), or imprisoned by the limitations of the water or astral plane. Two goddesses associated with the moon and the sea take care of him, or temporarily hide him and "veil" him in an underwater grotto.

Hephaestus was rejected from heaven (Olympus) due to his weakness and ugliness (qualities unbecoming a god). He was redeemed because of the beauty and fine workmanship of his craft. Nine years suggests initiation (a number D. K. often refers to in relationship to initiation). "At the first initiation, the disciple has to contend with the crystallizing and destroying forces of Vulcan and Pluto. The influences of Vulcan reaches to the very depths of his nature, whilst Pluto drags to the surface and destroys all that hinders in these lower regions" (Bailey, 1951, p. 70). Vulcan is the "forger of metals, the one who works in the densest, most concrete expression of the natural world (from the human angle). He is the one who goes down to the depths to find the material upon which to expand his innate art and to fashion that which is beautiful and useful" (Bailey, 1951, p. 385).

After the initiation or the first reconciliation between Hera and Hephaestus (Hephaestus has proved himself an able creator of beautiful forms that express something of the heaven world), he is once again rejected from Olympus. The second time it is the father or spirit aspect (Zeus) who repells him, indicating to him that a higher reconciliation (or initiation) must be brought about. Perhaps this relates to the higher initiation to which D. K. refers: "Vulcan is the ray or planet of isolation for . . . it governs the fourth initiation wherein the depths of aloneness are plumbed and the man stands completely isolated. He stands detached from that which is above and that which is below. There comes a dramatic moment when all desire is renounced; the will of God or the Plan is seen as the only desirable objective but as yet the man has not proved to himself, to the world of men or to his Master whether he has the strength to move forward along the line of service. There is revealed to him . . . some definite, active undertaking which embodies that aspect of the will of God which it is his peculiar function to appropriate and make possible of expression" (Bailey, 1951, p. 392).

The first separation from Olympus found Vulcan under the limitation of the Moon and the sea. At the second separation, he was a whole day in falling. In other words, it was a long way down, the separation between heaven and earth in his psychological state was great because he had climbed high and achieved much. There was no longer any astral plane to cushion his fall; he broke both legs as he fell on the island. He was "expelled" in a sense because he did not grasp the divine purpose and the will of God. This resulted in a state of acute isolation (an island) and the limitation not of the astral sea but of two broken legs. This suggests that the activity aspect as we normally think of it was greatly hampered, leaving the necessity to work primarily on the mental plane.

Generally speaking, we could say that there is a reference to the Vulcan energy at two levels:

Level One	Level Two
—first ray	—first ray
—first initiation—awakening to distance from the soul	—fourth initiation
—working beneath the sea, forced to overcome limita-	—awakening to distance from the Will of God (atma)

tions of astral plane
—reconciliation with Hera
  (form aspect)
—glorification of matter
  through detachment and
  purification
—uplift of matter
—beginning to use will
—developing strength, persistence, endurance
—destroying certain tenden-
  cies within oneself
—esoteric ruler Virgo and
  Taurus

—working with broken legs
  on an isolated island,
  forced to work in pure
  mental matter
—reconciliation with Zeus
  (here the father or will
  aspect)
—bending will of individual
  self to the greater Self
—pure spirit
—pure will, embodied will
—grasping divine purpose
—renouncing all desire
—hierarchical ruler Taurus

What is the meaning of the phrase "the glorification of matter through purification and detachment"? It is interesting that with Vulcan the form aspect is rightly utilized (glorified) rather than misused (Moon) or rejected (as initially done by Neptune). This, in part, can be attributed to the right use of the first ray as it deals with the physical plane and brings in the will—higher will or the sacrificial will of the soul. The personality with its egotism and selfishness brings about impurities and attachment, resulting in the defilement, rather than true glorification of matter. The energy of Vulcan helps to bring about a basic adjustment in one's attitude towards form-matter, enabling one to take the first initiation.

The first three initiations in D. K.'s system of esoteric psychology and developmental stages of soul unfoldment are related to the following factors:

First initiation. . . .overcoming maya. . . . .physical control
Second initiation. . .overcoming glamour. .emotional control
Third initiation. . . .overcoming illusion. . . .mental control

At the first initiation there is the work of demonstrating "control of the physical instrument" (Bailey, 1960, p. 588), of "resolving the dualities on the physical plane" and becoming "indifferent to the call or pull of matter" (Bailey, 1950, p. 103). "No one is accepted into the circle of the Ashram (which is the technical name given to the status of those who are on the eve of initiation or who are being prepared for initiation) whose physical appetites are in any danger of controlling him. This is a statement of fact. This applies particularly and specifically to those preparing for the first initiation" (Bailey, 1960, pp. 126–7). The first initiation should also "be regarded as instituting a new attitude towards relationships. . . . They embrace the recognition of those who must be served; they involve the expansion of the individual consciousness into a growing group awareness; they lead eventually to an eager response to hierarchical quality and to the magnetic pull of the Ashram" (Bailey, 1960, p. 668). It is also of interest that after the first initiation "the entire sex relationship shifts gradually and steadily into its proper place as simply a natural phase of existence in the three worlds and as one of the normal and correct appetites, but the emphasis changes. The higher experience and correspondence, that of which physical sex is only the symbol, becomes apparent. Instead of male and female, there emerges the magnetic relationship between the now negative personality and the positive soul, with consequent creativity upon the higher planes" (Bailey, 1960, pp. 668–9). The three initiations are also related to the transmutation of energy from the lower centers or chakras to the higher centers: sacral center to throat center, solar plexus to heart, and base of the spine to the head center. The first initiation is in part evidenced by the transferring of energy from the sacral to the throat. The sacral center is the center conditioning the sex relationship. The creative life then shifts from the sacral to the throat.

Hepheastus, the Blacksmith. Hepheastus (Vulcan) is described as being ugly, lame, ill-tempered, sooty-faced, horny-handed, and a hard-working man with powerful arms and shoulders. The mythological description characterizes somewhat the first ray influence, that is, strength and power, hard-working or a concentration upon physical plane work and necessities rather than emotional feelings and glamours. Hephaestus is a blacksmith, but that reference needs clarification. "It is not generally recognized that every Bronze Age tool, weapon or utensil had magical properties, and that the smith was something of a scorcerer. Thus, of the three persons of the Brigit Moon-triad [Moon goddesses], one presided over poets, another over smiths, the third over physicians" (Graves, 1955, p. 88). Archetypally, then, we can see the "smith" quality as a major attribute. The physician looked after the health and welfare of the physical body; the poet looked after the soul, the psychological world, the world of beauty, and the process of teaching through myth; and the smith, evidently, dealt with "ornamental and useful" objects—jewelry, tools, battle gear, weapons, mechanical devices, etc. The archetypes as characterized by ancient myth always have their contemporary equivalents. D. K. makes the interesting observation: "Vulcan also rules nations at a certain stage of embryonic soul expression, such as the present, and governs their activities, fashioning the instruments of war when war and conflict are the only means whereby liberation can come, though woe betide those through whom war comes" (Bailey, 1951, p. 386).

The "smith" then in an archetypal sense plays a far greater, more significant role than the word connotes to the contemporary world, generally speaking. The physician embodies a fifth ray, scientific quality. The poet embodies a fourth ray quality of harmony or beauty, related to the second ray of wisdom and teaching. The smith, as Vulcan, is related to the first ray of power—the fashioner of instruments of war, the one who works with the most difficult substance (the material most resistant to change)—with links to the seventh ray and the mineral kingdom.

Jane Addams' Dream: The Whole World Depended on Me Making a Wagon Wheel. The following dream (reported by Jane Addams in her autobiography *Twenty Years at Hull-House* seems to have captured much of the quality of Vulcan: "I dreamed night after night that every one in the world was dead excepting myself, and that upon me rested the responsibility of making a wagon wheel. The village street remained as usual, the village blacksmith shop was all there, even a glowing fire upon the forge and the anvil in its customary place near the door, but no human being was within sight. They had all gone around the edge of the hill to the village cemetery, and I alone remained in the deserted world. I always stood in the same spot in the blacksmith shop, darkly pondering as to how to begin, and never once did I know how, although I fully realized that the affairs of the world could not be resumed until at least one wheel should be made and something started. Every victim of nightmare is, I imagine, overwhelmed by an exces-

sive sense of responsibility and the consciousness of a
fearful handicap in the effort to perform what is required. The next morning would often find me, a deli-
cate little girl of six, with the further disability of a
curved spine, standing in the doorway of the village
blacksmith shop, anxiously watching the burly, red-
shirted figure at work. I would store my mind with
such details of the process of making wheels as I could
observe, and sometimes I plucked up courage to ask
for more. 'Do you always have to sizzle the iron in water?' I would ask, thinking how horrid it would be to
do. 'Sure!' the good-natured blacksmith would reply,
'that makes the iron hard.' I would sigh heavily and
walk away, bearing my responsibility as best I could,
and this of course I confided to no one, for there is
something too mysterious in the burden of 'the winds
that come from the fields of sleep' to be communi-
cated, although it is at the same time too heavy a burden to be borne alone" (Addams, 1910, pp. 5–6).

It is interesting that "everyone in the world was
dead excepting myself." This refers of course to consciousness, not form. People as physical entities and as
personalities can be "alive" in form but "dead" or un-
awakened in consciousness, relatively speaking. In the
dream the people had "died", and it was up to her to
get something started and moving again. Only she
was alive, that is, she had the highly responsible work
of quickening consciousness and rejuvenating life in
people who had slid into a mechanical, un-soul-
thinking existence. A crucial energy for the task allot-
ted her was that of Vulcan. The Vulcan energy has to
do with overcoming tenacious resistance through the
sacrificial will, persistence, and endurance. It has to
do with fashioning dense substance (human ignorance

or inertia, unawakenedness) into a holistic, principled vitality—organized for service. The symbol is the smithy who through strength (will) and knowledge makes indispensible objects, such as wagon wheels, enabling a right *activity* (rajas) to "go around" and to overcome inertia.

Jane Addams (1860–1935) did her work during the time that the United States, in the midst of an industrial revolution, had very few, if any, social services. Some of her labors included establishing a philanthropic community center. "From the first it seemed understood that we were ready to perform the humblest neighborhood services. We were asked to wash the new-born babies, and to prepare the dead for burial, to nurse the sick, and to mind the children," provide shelter for battered wives, to provide food for the unemployed, to offer culturally enriching activities (poetry readings, philosophical-social discussions, craft shops), and also living quarters and recreational activities. Other work dealt with bringing about changes in social legislation (child labor laws, workman's compensation, sanitary working conditions), and "spending many hours in efforts to secure support for deserted women, insurance for bewildered widows, damages for injured operators, furniture from the clutches of the installment store" (Addams, pp. 107, 109). Jane Addams served as a member of the Chicago Board of Education. She maintained three baths in the basement of Hull-House, since the tenements were without baths, and argued successfully for the building of the first public bathhouse in Chicago. She persuaded the Public Library Board to establish a branch reading room at Hull-House. A dramatic arts club was established. She arranged for college extension classes to be held at Hull-House, and at its peak the faculty numbered thirty-five. In 1909 she became the first woman president of the National Conference of Charities and Corrections, now the National Conference of Social Welfare. She led in the fight to give women the vote and was an ardent pacifist. She served as president of the Women's International League for Peace and Freedom, was the chairperson of the Woman's Peace Party, and in 1931 she was awarded the Nobel peace prize.

The first ray of Vulcan must have served her well, indeed, must have been indispensable in her work of "melting down" some stubbornly tenacious and selfish attitudes and refashioning the available energy-substance along more holistic lines—thus, enabling higher and subtler energies to circulate through the newly fashioned and truly serving forms. Physically somewhat frail as she might have been, nevertheless, she was a strong and powerful "smithy" indeed.

A Dream of Vulcan: The Shroud of the Moon Veiling Humble Service. Several years ago, while inquiring into the nature of Vulcan, and the meaning of the Moon veiling Vulcan, I had the following dream: *I, as a young man, was driving in a car with a police detective. He was showing me a part of the town that one usually doesn't see—a casual ride through the slums and back streets. But underneath the surface of things, it was more than that. I was being tested for a possible position. Would I see the problems that existed there? The detective casually pointed out a few things with no explanation. He pointed them out in such a way that if I chose to see them I could, but if I chose not to, the whole ride could pass as a minor and insignificant event.*

There was no pressure to see anything. Yet he observed me carefully for my reaction.

The scene changed. I was with an Englishman at a railroad crossing. A train was going by with several open, flat-bed cars. Strangely, the railroad cars became closer and closer to the ground until they were flush with the rails. This made it very easy to board the train. The Englishman and I jumped on, rode along, and arrived somehow in an European city. I wanted to ride on farther. The train stopped, and there we were, conspicuously out in the open, having obviously hitched a ride without buying a ticket. An officious person came along and looked at us in a scolding manner. We thought it best to get off.

We came to a restaurant. A waitress greeted us in a friendly manner. She seemed attracted to us. We were not sure where to sit. In many European restaurants there are often two or three sections with different prices. In one section there may be tables without cloths; in another section there may be tables with table cloths, better service, superior fare, etc. First I sat down in the least expensive section. Then I got up and moved to another section, then another. My English friend found a section that had good food but was still economical. Strangely enough, this section was without tables, let alone table cloths. I waved him over to another section. "Let's sit at a table," I said. "It's not everyday I'm in Europe. Let's enjoy it."

In the meantime the waitress introduced us to her younger sister. The younger sister joined us, while the older sister went about her duties. The younger sister told us how beautiful the Moon was. As she described the Moon, I listened closely, for I knew it wasn't the time of the full Moon and I was wondering what sort of differentiation she was trying to make. She said that the Moon had a "dress", which struck me as an inappropriate word. I asked her to say it in her native tongue, which by then I knew was German. As she described the Moon in German, I realized that she was reciting a German poem, and that the poet had compared the Moon to a young woman. I suggested that the word "shroud" might be a more appropriate word in English for the German word "Kleid", because "shroud" was more poetic and "dress" seemed inappropriately commonplace. The younger sister was romantically touched by this description of the Moon. She seemed to be a person who could hardly wait for the evening to come in order to see the Moon and be enraptured by it. The older sister was busy waiting on tables and serving customers. The younger sister only appeared when there was fun and romance at hand. The striking thing about relating to her was that she was conversing with something else—an image perhaps of astral, romantic pleasantries. The envelop of imagery prevented her from seeing the other, herself, and the situation.

In the dream we have three scenes that are unrelated in form but related in quality. In the first scene there is presented the possibility of a new level of awareness, or expansion of consciousness, to include "new" qualitative energies, namely, the first ray. The new energy has to do with becoming aware of problems that one tends to avoid and not recognize. We are asked to look with open eyes at dire effects that include some suffering and pain. We are in a position, however, in which we can choose between assuming a more responsible labor or remaining closed to certain unpleasant "realities."

The next scene is a transitional one. There is a "crossing", suggesting crisis-conflict or choice opportunity. There is an ease of transition (flush rails, easy to board). There is even a free ride (or should we say, "free lunch"?). The transition is one on metal rails—a Vulcan symbol. We are not travelling here by sea or air. We are travelling by earth, rendered usable by fire. (It is interesting to note that Vulcan is given as the esoteric ruler of two Earth signs, Taurus and Virgo). We are aided in this transition by an Englishman. England, according to D. K., has a first ray personality. The first ray English tend to be very conscious of class, of propriety, protocol, of doing everything in the socially and class conscious correct way. We are allowed to break the law and have a free ride up to a point—but no farther. We are allowed to journey on our way, riding primarily on the sweat and labor of others—but only to a point.

The third and final scene presents the problem and difficulty. "I wanted to ride on farther", but we had to get off. Why Europe? I spent my early twenties in Europe. It represents to me several things: a crisis time when I was desperately, one might say, in search of the soul. It also represents culture and depth of tradition and thought. I felt at the time more artistically and spiritually "at home" in Europe than I did in the United States. The dream suggests a "crossing of the great water", that is, a significant crisis-transition period, albeit the crossing was made on earth and rail. The Englishman, with his polite and proper recognition of the power factor, knew what rule could be broken and which ones had to be obeyed. Up to the point of table-and-section selection, I followed the Englishman's lead. He chose a section without table. How can one eat without a table? My deciding point was an enjoyment factor. The Englishman's point then was a Spartan one—simplicity, discipline and bare necessity. The enjoyment factor leads right into the veil of the Moon. One might say that one enjoyment leads to another, and another. One's consciousness can be enveloped by a series of mild enjoyments and indulgences. This can lead to subtly or not so subtly self-destructive habits and addictions. Innocent enough they seem initially. There is always the rational that will find some acceptable reason, such as: "It's not everyday that I'm in Europe."

In the restaurant there are two sisters. One is a waitress—she humbly serves. The other is unemployed. She has *no real work*. She is enraptured by the cover of darkness and the Moon's reflected light. She is the epitome of the veil of the Moon. She does not know love, because she does not truly love. Love is a giving, a reciprocation, a self-sacrificing, an ability to see the other, a working together with another. Of these things she wants no part. While she proclaims love, her romantic mood veils love. In her presence one has the feeling that should her romantic love alight upon you like a cute and hungry chickadee during winter's sparse pickings, you know that come along spring's new vegetation she'll alight quickly elsewhere, as if she never knew you.

The "dress" of the Moon, the garment of the Moon, is an adornment and a veil. Poetry at one level awakens us to Beauty and reveals Truth. On another level poetry can be a means of veiling rather than revealing. It can generate glamours rather than disperse them. It can lead astray under the guise of beauty. It can generate a false astral light. "Shroud" is defined as a "white cloth or sheet in which a corpse is laid for burial." The word is supposed to describe the Moon in a poetic way, but unwittingly "shroud" reveals the romantic mood-illusion for what it is—a path towards death, that is, a path of wrong relationship with its subtle destructiveness rather than a path towards love. It masquerades as love. Love is acceptable. Love is admired. Love is loved. So what is *not* love, we call love, thereby rendering it acceptable, at least for the moment. The dream dramatizes just one of many ways in which the Moon can veil Vulcan. For some the veil is related to a distortion of love. For others the veil may be related to a distortion of other ray energies—power, wisdom, activity (busy-ness), money, intellect, knowledge, devotion (to person, organization or idea), to beauty, to organizational abilities, as well as a host of sub-divisions of the above.

Vulcan and the Average Man. D. K. has suggested, as mentioned in the first paragraph of this essay, that astrologers "work with Vulcan when dealing with the undeveloped or average man and with Uranus when considering the highly developed man." With that in mind, we might try to summarize the Vulcan indications given in the dream.

1. Vulcan's first ray influence prods us to look behind the scenes, to look more deeply at the desire, personal-will factor, to penetrate to that aspect of reality that looks squarely at unpleasant effects of society's basically selfish orientation, and then to take some responsibility in altering the condition.
2. Responsibility begins with a close scrutiny of one's own desire life. It is necessary to look ruthlessly at

how one's own consciousness is veiled by the Moon.

3. Vulcan has a Spartan influence. It brings a self-discipline which includes a destruction of those factors that prevent the expansion of the soul life through the personality. It brings a meaningful and purposeful simplicity that replaces the unnecessary complexity of personality life.

4. If Uranus and the seventh ray via the initiate can change the world, then Vulcan in its initial stages can begin to change the world by changing oneself.

5. There is a fundamental "evolutionary urge", a will, required to offset the potent forces of inertia and the established form.

As well as suggesting that astrologers work with "Vulcan when dealing with the undeveloped or average man", D. K. also tells us that "Vulcan is never an exoteric ruler and only comes into real activity when a man is on the Path" (Bailey, 1951, p. 509). These statements may at first appear contradictory, but on closer examination there is no contradiction. Vulcan is a key energy in offsetting the influence of the Moon. The ordinary person needs to *begin* to work with this energy as glamour is confronted and inertia overcome. But Vulcan *never rules* exoterically. The energy is never fully developed and the person never completely compatible with it at the personality level. Only as a soul, when the person is "on the Path", does it come into "real activity." It seems to me that Jane Addams is a good example of the Vulcan energy functioning at the soul level.

It can be noted from the list of exoteric and esoteric planetary rulers (see appendix) that in connection with ordinary man there are no first ray planetary rulers. In connection with advanced man (and the esoteric rulers) there are three signs in which we find a first ray planetary ruler: Taurus (Vulcan), Virgo (Moon veiling Vulcan), and Pisces (Pluto).

Interestingly, Jane Addams had her Sun in Virgo. It might be of value to researchers in esoteric astrology to look for pronounced types of the Vulcan influence among those who have Taurus or Virgo as Sun or rising signs. The Vulcan influence would certainly not be limited to those particular cases. It seems to me that during the months of Taurus and Virgo the first ray of Vulcan is uniquely available to anybody able to tap the esoteric levels of energy to some degree.

Vulcan's "location" (if we can use that three-dimensional term when referring to the "hidden" planets on etheric and higher levels) may be close to the Sun. "Vulcan is a substitute for the Sun; it is spoken of sometimes as being veiled by the Sun and at others it stands for the Sun itself. It stands between the man and the Sun, the soul." "Vulcan has hitherto been hidden, but its influence has steadily superseded all lunar control, for the personality or form side of life is lost to sight in the radiance of the Sun, the soul. The light of Vulcan and the light of the Sun are one light and these three—Mercury, Vulcan and the Sun—stand for a synthesis and a radiance which eventually dims the light of Mercury and it 'falls' into the background and Vulcan too becomes invisible and only the Sun remains" (Bailey, 1951, pp. 393, 132).

In our efforts to understand the hints and suggestions given in *Esoteric Astrology*, it is vital to recognize the various *levels* to which D. K. is referring. The above paragraph refers to several levels (perhaps three) of vastly different states of consciousness, or dif-

ferent levels of initiation into the planetary and systemic life. The three levels suggested are:

1. Vulcan veiled by Sun (as personality). Intermediary
   between personality and Sun (as soul). Vital energy
   in releasing one from lunar control (control by
   form).
2. Vulcan and Sun as one. Soul consciousness, Synthesis of Vulcan, Sun and Mercury.
3. Only the Sun remains. The pure spiritual will. The
   spirit of man (rather than soul), the monadic being,
   alignment with the Central Spiritual Sun. Interme-
   diaries of Vulcan and Mercury no longer needed.

The level that we have focused on in this essay is obviously the first level—humanity's initial acquaintance
with the first ray Vulcan as one opts for release from
form control, or should we say form addiction. In order
to deal with the third or form aspect (which includes
personality), in order to loosen its pervasive control
over the consciousness of man, an act of will is required.

Vulcan and the Para-Thyroid Chakra. We find another most interesting passage in *Esoteric Astrology*
regarding the Vulcan energy and influence. In discussing the centers (chakras) and planets, D. K. mentions
that the Sun, standing in this case for the sacred
planet Vulcan, "governs a center in the front of the
throat which is related to the para-thyroids and not to
the thyroid gland, which is related to the throat center. This center in the front of the throat falls into
disuse as the creative period of throat activity begins.
It acts as a 'mediator' between the higher and the

lower creative organs (between the sacral and the throat centers) and leads eventually to that creative activity which is consciously that of the functioning soul. Vulcan was one of the first creative workers among men. He was also related to 'Cain who killed his brother.' The symbolism underlying these ancient myths will be easily interpreted by the intuitive student" (Bailey, 1951, pp. 78-9).

We have already touched upon Vulcan as one of the first creative workers. As mentioned, in ancient Greece the poet, physician and "smithy" held special prominence. Fashioning instruments of war, utilitarian gadgets, as well as decorative and commemorative jewelry and statues, etc., requires a creative energy. The energy required is something more than what is available from the three major lower centers—base of spine, sacral and solar plexus. It stands to reason that one of the first creative workers would be related to the physical plane in a practical and utilitarian sort of way. But at the same time it requires a slaying of an aspect of oneself and it begins to relate one to the higher worlds. Again, the work of Jane Addams is creative in that "the affairs of the world could not be resumed until at least one wheel should be made and something started."

"The energy of the sacral center governing the sexual life and the organs of physical creation must be raised to the throat center, which becomes the organ of creative activity of a non-physical nature" (Bailey, 1942, p. 523). "The creative physical urge is transmuted into artistic or literary creation in some form or another, and later still into the power to create groups or organizations which will express some idea or some thought which emanates from the Mind of God, and

which demands immediate precipitation upon earth"
(Bailey, 1942, p. 390). Vulcan as a mediator between
the higher and the lower creative organs suggests a
temporary act of will necessary to redirect activity
leading eventually to its stabilization on a higher, subtler, more abstract, more principled level.

Summary. For purposes of recapitulation and conve-
nient reference, our summary list is divided into three
categories: (1) the Moon, (2) the veiling phenomenon,
and (3) the Vulcan energy.

The Moon
—a dead form, no emanation, no radiation, no quality
—has powerful astral and thought effect
—disintegrating physically
—limitations, handicaps of the past
—inertia, tamasic aspect
—prison of the soul
—corruption, decay, injurious emanations
—instinct
—lunar lords, builders of the form
—vampirizing the earth
—symbol of astral and lower manas (concrete mind)

The Veiling Phenomenon
—veiled or hidden planet refers to non-physical planet
  (etheric, astral or mental)
—the Moon (limitations of past and form) veils higher planetary and systemic influences
—a subtle mental block
—an erroneous thought that prevents soul relationship
—imprisoning attitude
—illusion of knowing
—distorted perception generated by personal self-
  centeredness

The Vulcan Energy
—first ray of power and will
—intense labor
—related to first initiation
—glorification of matter through purification and detachment
—endurance aspect of the will-to-be
—persistence, continuity of effort
—supersedes all lunar control
—release from bondage of form (Moon)
—forger of metals
—works in most concrete expression of physical plane
—fashions what is beautiful and useful
—related also to fourth initiation
—depths of aloneness, completely isolated
—renouncing all desire
—substituting right labor (beautiful and useful) for appetite
—service attitude towards relationships
—hard and unglamorous work
—willing to perform the humblest tasks
—fashioner of instruments of war
—rules Earth signs Taurus and Virgo esoterically
—Spartan-like self-discipline
—purposeful simplicity
—an evolutionary urge, a will-to-be, that offsets inertia
—governs etheric chakra related to parathyroids
—mediator between sacral and throat chakras (lower and higher creative organs)
—leads to soul creativity through act of will

The Sun Veils Neptune

In *Esoteric Astrology* it is indicated that the Sun, as well as the Moon, "veils" certain planets. The three planets that are mentioned by name (in reference to both the Sun and the Moon) are Vulcan, Neptune, and Uranus. Consider the following statement: "The Sun veils certain hidden planets, and in the case of Leo, the two planets through which the Sun focuses its energy or influence (like a lens) are Neptune and Uranus. The 'heart of the Sun' employs Neptune as its agent, whilst the central, spiritual Sun pours its influence through Uranus" (p. 296).

We have, then, three levels of energy designated by the Sun as "ruler of all three conditions of Leo":

1. exoteric. . . . . . .Sun   3.
2. estoeric. . . . . . .Heart of Sun . . . . .veiling Neptune 2.
3. hierarchical . . .Central, Spiritual Sun. . .veiling Uranus 1.

31

Our effort in this essay is to get some practical understanding of what these three levels mean, with a particular focus on that second condition of the "Sun veiling Neptune."

Beginning with the first condition, we could consider the meaning of the Sun in Leo. "It is a correct surmise that the purpose of this solar system is the unfoldment of consciousness, and if for the human being self-consciousness is the goal, then the Sun must obviously rule, for it is the source of physical consciousness (exoteric and symbolic of personality), of soul awareness (esoteric), and of spiritual life (hierarchical). . . . The outstanding theme of Leo is the activity of the self-conscious unit in relation to its environment or *the development of sensitive response to surrounding impacts* by the one who stands—as the Sun stands—at the center of its little universe. The whole story and function of Leo and its influence can be summed up in the word *'sensitivity'* and this sensitivity can be studied in four stages:

1. Sensitivity to conditioning impacts from the environment, i.e., to the impacts of the world of human evolution. . . .
2. Sensitivity to the will, wishes and desires of the personality, the integrated self-conscious man, the lower self.
3. Sensitivity to the soul as the conditioning factor instead of sensitivity to the environing world as the conditioning factor.
4. The spiritual sensitivity of the God-Man (the soul and personality fused) to the environment. At this stage of unfoldment, the liberated man is not conditioned by his environment but begins the arduous task of conditioning it in relation to the divine

plan and purpose and at the same time to culti-
vating sensitivity to the higher impacts of those
worlds which lead to the final goal" (Bailey, 1951,
pp. 294-5).

In the first solar system the purpose dealt with
the development of form (the third aspect). In the next
or third solar system there will be the unfoldment of
the will (first aspect). But presently the focus is on the
consciousness or sentient aspect (the second). For purposes of clarity the consciousness aspect can be viewed
in terms of three aspects:

Exoteric. . . . .Sun . . . .environmental . . . . . personality
                     impacts   development
Esoteric. . . . .Neptune .sensitivity to soul. . . soul development
                     and intuitional levels
Hierarchical .Uranus. .spiritual sensitivity. . development of
                                      the God-Man

Further correspondences:

Physical Sun. . . . . .personality. . . .self-consciousness
Heart of Sun. . . . . .soul. . . . . .group consciousness
Central Spiritual Sun . .monad . . . . . . .God consciousness

D. K. refers to the Heart of the Sun as the "subjective Sun" which "influences the soul" (p. 147) and
"reveals the nature of the soul" (p. 620). The *physical*
Sun, then, is a *form* manifestation of a subjective being, a Solar Logos. In way of perhaps rather crude
analogy and considering the three aspects of personality, a child first becomes acquainted with the *physical*
environment of his parents, later can enter somewhat
in to the *emotional* life of the parents as he absorbs

and participates in their set of values, and eventually can appreciate and relate on *mental* levels and in the intellectual life. Each developmental stage has its primary focus on one of these levels, though all three levels are always present and influencing. There is an analogy here, then, to the Solar Life. One might say that the human tendency to think of the Sun only as a physical entity is indicative of that human stage during which self-consciousness and personality are developed. A child, as well as being loved, must be protected and restricted. This, in a sense, is the work of Saturn, as necessary limits are sometimes painfully imposed on childlike, personality developing man. Saturn is "one of the most potent of the four Lords of Karma and forces man to face up to the past, and in the present to prepare for the future" (Bailey, 1951, p. 164). It is in another related sense, however, all the exoteric planetary influences that provide the psychological environing conditions that limit and rear childlike, personality man.

In view of the above, we might consider the following very general analogies or correspondences:

Exoteric....Sun ....Activity cycle......1st Solar System
  rulers   of early years   form manifestation
Esoteric....Heart...Conscious deeping ..2nd Solar System
  rulers   of Sun   of middle years   consciousness
                                            development
Hierarchical.Central..Power, will........3rd Solar System
  rulers   Spiritual refinement   will-power
              Sun   of mature years

One might say that the heart of this solar system is to develop the heart-soul-consciousness aspect. The unveiled Neptune, as it reveals the Heart of the Sun, must then be a very key factor in evolution and the development of consciousness. Up to this point it has been stated that Neptune, in this sense, has to do with:

—unfolding consciousness
—soul awareness
—sensitivity to the soul
—bridge towards God-Man
—reveals nature of soul

If we recall the work of Vulcan, as veiled by the Moon, we will quickly see that Neptune's work, as it relates to the human family, is far different. The "blacksmith" is much different, in terms of energy employed, from the "mystic-poet"—in the archetypal sense.

The Real Sun, the Heart of the Sun. "The real Sun under which our planetary life will eventually function and to which response will be made is the Heart of the Sun. When that is controlling, the spiritual man will then live a dual life simultaneously and this dual life will consist of our apparent experience and situations and our inner spiritual soul awareness. The personality will still respond to influences coming to it from the physical Sun but the motivated life activity and the subjective experience of the inner man will be conditioned by energies coming to him from the 'Heart of the Sun.' I would here recall to your minds the teaching of the Ageless Wisdom as given in the *Secret Doctrine* and elaborated in my later books, that the Sun has to be discovered and known in its triple nature, which is threefold as is the Trinity" (Bailey, 1951, pp. 110–111).

Here we have another interesting clue as to what is meant by the "Heart of the Sun" and the possible role that Neptune might be playing. The physical Sun is not the "real" or total Sun in an analogous sense that the physical body of a person is not the real person. Or more accurately, the physical heart and the etheric heart center are not the real person or being but simply vital organs that transmit energy.

Plato's Cave Analogy. Plato's Cave analogy might help us understand and appreciate part of the Neptunian influence and help us understand the interplay, the dialectic, between the real and the unreal, the world of appearance and the world of quality, between form and consciousness, between the physical light source and the inner light source. Socrates, in Plato's *Republic,* asks us to take the "following parable of education and ignorance as a picture of the condition of our nature." Socrates describes a situation in which people are chained in a cave in such a way that they are only able to look upon one side of the cave wall. Behind them and higher up at a distance is a fire burning. Between the people and the fire are "bearers" who carry all sorts of things, one after the other, in a kind of procession. The chained people, or "prisoners", see only the shadows cast on the cave wall. The task of the prisoners becomes that of naming the projected shadows, believing as they do that they are actually naming real things. Socrates then asks us what it would be like if a prisoner were released from his chains? Would he not be "dazzled to see distinctly those things whose shadows he had seen before? What do you think he would say, if someone told him that what he saw before was foolery, but now he saw more rightly, being a bit nearer reality and turned towards what was a little more real? What if he were shown each of the passing things and compelled by questions to answer what each one was? Don't you think he would be puzzled, and believe what he saw before was more true than what was shown to him now?" We are then asked to suppose that the freed prisoner is forced to leave the cave and emerge into the real light. "When he came into the light, the brilliance would fill his eyes and he would not be able to see even one of the things now called real." In stages his eyes would adjust and he would look at shadows, then at water, then at things themselves and, lastly, at the sun.

Among his prisoner friends below in the cave, it was the custom to give honours, praises and prizes to those who "saw the passing things most sharply and remembered best which of them used to come before and which together, and from these was best able to prophesy accordingly what was going to come." But what would happen if the freed prisoner returned to the cave to help his friends? His eyes would take time to adjust to darkness. "And if he should have to compete with those who had been always prisoners, by laying down the law about those shadows while he was blinking before his eyes were settled down, wouldn't they all laugh at him and say he had spoiled his eyesight by going up there, and it was not worth-while so much as to try to go up? And would they not kill anyone who tried to release them and take them up, if they could somehow lay hands on him and kill him?"

Socrates goes on to explain some factors in the analogy. Normal sight and everyday life is comparable to imprisonment and the observation of shadows. The fire is analogous to our physical sun. "The ascent and the view of the upper world is the rising of the soul into the world of mind." Those who returned from the upper world are "not willing to have part in the affairs of men, but their souls ever strive to remain above." And Socrates asks, "Do you think it surprising if one leaving divine contemplations and passing to the evils of man is awkward and appears to be a great fool, while he is still blinking—not yet accustomed to the darkness around him, but compelled to struggle in law courts or elsewhere about shadows of justice, or the images which make the shadows, and to quarrel about notions of justice in those who have never seen justice itself?"

Socrates also explains that just as the prisoner could see nothing but shadows, until his whole body was turned from the dark to the light, similarly, the "instrument [by which one learns] must be turned round with the whole soul away from the world of becoming until it is able to endure the sight of becoming and the most brilliant light of being."

We have three conditions or stages presented in the analogy. The first condition is one of being imprisoned or psychologically "caught" in the shadowy world of appearance. This is the "normal" condition. This is the everyday situation of human personalities. Everyone at this level judges one another by one's ability to differentiate one's own favorite set of shadows. Whatever one has happened to learn of this transient and constantly changing world, that then will also be his point of measurement of others.

The second condition has to do with being relatively disentangled from the fetters binding one to the world of shadows-appearances and rising to the insight of something which has been called light, a higher world, a greater dimension or greater reality. Initially, it is an experience of an inner light, insight, a new vision of things as they more truly are, a trancendentally and expansively new awareness, etc. The Neptunian energy brings about this basically mystical and intuitive experience. Perception moves to the real and away from the unreal. The whole is seen. The light source is seen. And the Greater Light and higher worlds are cognized. Socrates, or Plato, describes the experience as being "dazzled to see distinctly those things whose shadow he had seen before." In order to comprehend the dimension above, an analogous picture is presented of a dimension below. We know that shadows are not the real thing. The real thing casts shadows. Shadows are, in themselves, without substance, though they appear to be substantial. Things as we perceive them are truly like shadows and not the real thing in themselves. In order to comprehend the shadows we must see the higher worlds that give rise to the play of "shadows" or world of appearances. Socrates explains: "The ascent and the view of the upper world is the rising of the soul into the world of mind" (W. H. D. Rouse's translation). Familiar as we are with the Tibetan's terminology, it might be more accurate to say: the rising of the *mind* into the world of *soul.* After all, the intellectual analysis of the shadows is there (the lower, concrete mind). It is the rising of that mind to, or the alignment of that mind with the soul (on the higher mental plane, the arupa aspect of the fifth plane) that occurs.

The third condition deals with the unfettered man in relationship to those imprisoned by the world

of appearances. Those who return from the upper
world are "not willing to have part in the affairs of
men, but their souls ever strive to remain above."
Once again we can see that in a sense this Neptunian
stage is very similar to the crucified Christ. Indeed,
why return to a shadowy world where the "last among
you will be first and the first among you will be last",
where prizes are often given for shadowy accomplish-
ments, and where light-bearers are often ridiculed and
sometimes crucified. How is one to loosen the chains
when the prisoners themselves do not want to be set
free? How can one expand minds when the fettered
ones display such inertia and resistance? Indeed, how
can one love, when love is hated? Frightful and shock-
ing situation, indeed, to the Neptunian soul who is
"striving to remain above." But return he must, for it
is the law.

It is obvious that at this third condition or stage
something more than the Neptunian influence is
needed. Neptune, esoterically speaking—with its sixth
ray energy (idealistic perception), with its second ray
relationship to the Heart of the Sun, and with its
fourth ray connection with buddhi (the plane of
intuition)—is that energy which aids in the revelation
process and seeing of the vision. The eye of vision is
able to detect aspects of the Plan of God. Neptune
helps to remove the fetters of the world of appearances
as it kindles aspiration to the world of meaning. But
the two-four-six line of ray energies is insufficient in
many ways for altering the shadowy state of affairs. In
Plato's words, the fetters are not innate. Indeed, the
children are close to their souls. There are certain
"leaden weights", however, which "grow into the soul

from gorging and gluttony and such pleasures, and twist the soul's eye downwards." These weights, however, could be "hammered at since childhood," so that "higher things" could be seen more clearly. Plato is espousing a sort of right and spiritually aligned education. "Then it is the task of us founders to compel the best natures to attain that learning which we said was the greatest, both to see the good, and to ascend that ascent; and when they have ascended and properly seen, we must never allow them . . . to stay there and not be willing to descend again to those prisoners, and to share their troubles and their honours, whether they are worth having or not. . . . Down you must go then, in turn, to the habitation of the others, and accustom yourselves to their darkness; for when you have grown accustomed you will see a thousand times better than those who live there, and you will know what the images are and what they are images of, because you have seen the realities behind just and beautiful and good things. And so our city will be managed wide awake for us and for you, not in a dream, as most men are now, by people fighting together for shadows, and quarrelling to be rulers, as if that were a great good" (Plato, *Great Dialogues of Plato,* trans. W. H. D. Rouse, pp. 312, 313, 315, 316, 317, 318, 319).

Plato's analogy of the cave, with its three level-stages, seems to have correspondences to the "veiled" planetary rulers under discussion. The breaking of the fetters, requiring an act of will, corresponds to our first acquaintance with Vulcan. Perceiving the real, which lies behind the unreality of the shadowy world of appearances, corresponds to the mystical and envisioning stage of Neptune. At this stage the advanced person or disciple longs to "remain above" and often does not want to take part in the affairs of men." The third stage deals with the initiate consciousness and Uranian influence in the esoteric sense. Here the initiate must accustom him/herself to the darkness and shadows, and must "share their troubles and honours" and labor to loosen the fetters of others and bring in the light.

These three stages compare well to the levels of sensitivity mentioned in the early part of the essay:

1. Sensitivity to personality . . The Sun, the Hidden Christ,
   the lower self   fettered by form, appearance.
2. Sensitivity to the soul . . . . . Neptune, Heart of Sun,
                                    Crucified Christ, development
                                    of mystic and intuitive sense,
                                    envisioning the Plan.
3. Spiritual sensitivity
   of God-Man . . . . Uranus, Central Spiritual Sun,
   begins arduous   Living Risen Christ, use of the
   task of conditioning the   spiritual will.
   environment in relation to
   the divine plan and purpose.

The Factor of Veiling. How does the Sun "veil" Neptune? What is the meaning of the term "veiling"? The Sun as a physical celestial body does not veil or hide the physical planet Neptune. The phrase "the Sun veils Neptune" cannot be taken literally; it does not refer to a physical phenomenon. If not a physical factor, then it must refer to a consciousness factor. If not outer, then inner. "The Sun veils Neptune" is meant metaphorically or symbolically. That is to say, a very real energy state, or developmental stage of consciousness, is denoted by the cryptic phrase: "the Sun veils Neptune."

The Sun as a non-sacred planet is a symbol of personality and has to do with the powerful illusion of being the one at the center. The personal consideration veils the group good. The group good, the good of the whole, is not recognized nor appreciated by the one who blatantly or subtly, overtly or covertly, places the personal accretion before the releasing principle. The illusion of being the one at the center conditions all aspects of personality life, resulting in ignorance, conflict, wars, dis-ease, pain, suffering, etc. The veil lifts as the center shifts. What was once central becomes peripheral.

There are a number of ways in which we could try to appreciate this most interesting phenomenon. I recall a friend of mine who was working in a scientific field and was one of the top researchers in his speciality. We were discussing certain unconventional and intriguing directions of research. His final word on the matter was: "But I can't follow that direction, because I'd be putting my scientific reputation on the line." From a personality point of view, we are talking about a risky situation, indeed. After all, my scientific friend had received the laurels of his profession. His articles were published in the trade journals, he had an important position at a leading institute, he was asked to chair meetings at international conferences, etc. All that hard won territory would indeed be on the line. One might say that he had a choice between his reputation on the one hand and truth on the other. Or one could say that his choice was between personal well-being (the Sun) and pursuing those subtle directions towards soul (Neptune). Esoteric Neptune invites us to place truth in a central position, but at what a risk. Who will walk that path of self-sacrifice, of relinquishment, of insecurity, of unconventionality, of ridicule—and, as Socrates pointed out, even death?

Another friend of mine made an interesting comment that has stayed with me for many years. In our youth and in our course of studies we used to *dream* of doing great things (as Neptune likes us to do). There were those great examples in our history and literature courses that lent concretion to our *imaginings.* "But look at how they suffered," I said, "and look how recognition wasn't their's in their lifetime." His comment was, "You have to be just *ten* years ahead of your time," the implication being that somehow one could have a firm foot in both worlds. One could supposedly be ahead of one's times, but not be so far ahead that one did not receive the recognition, the laurels, etc. In such a case, however, there would be no true decentralization from personality. As personality manipulates truth for its own personal benefit, then the veil still blocks the path via Neptune to the Heart of the Sun. Aspiration is part of Neptune's realm, but when aspiration is filled with selfish intent, the veil is not lifted. Attachments still fetter one to the world of shadows. One cannot yet be trusted to use Knowledge only to benefit and not to harm one's group brothers.

"Karl Pribram recalls the remark of a pioneer memory researcher, Ewald Hering, that at some point in his life, every scientist must make a decision. 'He begins to be interested in his work and what his findings mean,' Pribram said. 'Then he has to choose. If he starts to ask questions and tries to find answers, to understand what it all means, he will look foolish to his colleagues. On the other hand, he can give up the attempt to understand what it all means; he won't look foolish, and he'll learn more and more about less and less. You have to decide to have the courage to look foolish" (Marilyn Ferguson, "Karl Pribram's Changing Reality").

"The famous physicist, Niels Bohr, once said that when the great innovations appear, it will seem muddled and strange. It will be only half understood by its discoverer and a mystery to everyone else. For any idea that does not appear bizarre at first, there is no hope" (Ferguson).

The "Sun veils Neptune" identifies the psychological principle. Examples illustrating it are countless.

An Experience of "the Veil." It is interesting to actually experience the subtle sensation of a "veil" or "film" that makes things appear to be one way, when in fact or in reality they are different, and often the exact opposite. I recall vividly one such sensation that has to do with relationship and loneliness. As people relate to each other as personalities, there is an attempt to find a certain acceptance and togetherness to off-set the sense of loneliness. Those who like to be alone follow the same pattern when they do relate, that is, they seek validation in relationship. As personalities we seek love, acceptance, validation, recognition, respect, etc. We seek these attitudes from others, but we are very reluctant to give them to others. When we do give them, it is often in an effort to receive something in return. Seldom do we find an enriching mutual interplay. Even when there appears to be mutual love, respect, etc., we find hollow and deep spaces of uncertainty in the relationship. We find a

need for reassurance and again for reassurance. When
the "veil" is lifted, however, it is an entirely different
story. Elevated to soul consciousness and soul relationship, we see how personality has placed a veil between
every relationship. It goes something like this: As
personalities we interact and become busy with inter-
action and have several friends and many acquaint-
ances, but we are always alone. As a soul, however, we
have no one with whom we can interact because they
are all clouded by personality. We appear to be quite
alone, yet conscious of soul, we are in fact never alone.
Behind the veil is the loneliness and the false activity
to counteract that sense of aloneness. When the veil is
lifted there is true and right relationship, which is difficult to describe because it is not within the limitation of time and space and the duality-polarity of that
realm. On the other hand, it is easy to describe because it is quite simple, much simpler than the com-
plexities of personality relationships. The personality
strives for something, and its moments of achievement
and consummation are fleeting. Soul, on the other
hand, does not ask the question of achievement and
consummation, for that presupposes separation. The
soul is not deficient in love or being. Also the soul relates soul to soul, which is not limited to time and
space. The soul does not say: I cannot relate to this
person because this person is enmeshed in personality
and unable to achieve my level. On the contrary, the
soul relates to the person's soul—or simply to soul.
Thus, there _is_ relationship now, and it is right relationship as it is soul to soul. The personality may be
befuddled by it, may feel only a silence, may hear
stimulating words, may be precipitated into a crisis,
may have itself mirrored back to it, may suddenly find
silently the answer one has been looking for within

oneself, etc. Whatever the personality reaction, it is not personality to whom the soul has primary relationship. The soul-soul relationship is there now, although in time and space the personality may only become conscious of it at a much later date.

The Necessity of the Temporary Limitation of Veiling. The factor of veiling, the illusion of the "I" consciousness and of being the one at the center, seems to serve some protective function during "youth" stages or form-developing stages. Apparently a certain individuality and self-awareness must be reached in order for the subtler, group oriented energies to be used in a proper and safe fashion.

In the discussion of the sign Cancer and in reference to the esoteric planetary ruler Neptune, D. K. writes: "In the mass mind (of which Cancer is the truest expression), it is fortunate that Neptune is veiled by the Moon and that the form fails to register or step down many of the impacts to which the true man is sensitive. Average humanity is not yet fully equipped to bear the full range of these impacts, to handle them constructively or to transmute them and interpret them accurately. Upon the Path of Discipleship and along the line of esoteric development, one of the major difficulties and great problems of the disciple is his extreme sensitivity to impacts from every side and his rapid ability to respond to contacts coming from 'all points of the compass, from every angle of the zodiacal wheel and from that which is within as well as from that which is without, from that which lies above, below, and upon every hand' " (Bailey, 1951, p. 322).

Veiling, then, serves a purpose in that it prevents "the full range of impacts" coming from "all points of the compass." The Neptunian quality greatly in-

Neptune overlaps

creases one's sensitivity, indeed, develops into "extreme sensitivity" to energies hitherto unrecognized. There are a number of ways in which we could appreciate this point. Mass consciousness is hardly sensitive to the greater principles, to group responsibility, or to the larger issues. Mass consciousness, as experienced by the individual, is concerned with its own personal happiness. As a result, vis-à-vis the larger issues, it goes "whichever way the wind blows." Even when fighting for a principle, the mass-conscious person is really being directioned by leaders and demagogs. The mass-conscious person says in effect: Don't make me think these things through, rather tell me what I should believe in.

If the energies cannot be handled "constructively," then there would be the tendency to handle them destructively or to misuse them in some fashion. Alan Leo remarks: "In some cases, again, that have come under our observation, Neptune represents a pure and chaste sex life, and exalted and purified love nature. So sublime are the vibrations of this planet that only the few can raise their consciousness to its level of expression; for its dual nature . . . causes it to be expressed in its highest only through the finest vehicles; therefore the mind and body must be pure, and well under control, before the higher and psychical expression can be manifest in the flesh" (Alan Leo, *Art Synthesis*, p. 105). "To come under the true influx of this planet's nature means spiritual awakening of the highest kind; to be under the dark side is enthrallment of the fleshly senses" (A. Leo, p. 118).

The use and misuse of drugs for mind-expanding and mood-elevating purposes has long been attributed to Neptune by orthodox astrologers. Some of the initial experiments with drugs were carried out by writers, artists, thinkers, who, one might say, were exploring ways of increasing their sensitivity to the inner and invisible worlds. In spite of the faulty experiments, some of the seekers were true candidates for developing the Neptunian energy. Their experiments had an element of increasing knowledge of unknown realms rather than personal satisfaction. As the experiments trickled down to the masses, however, extensive damage occurred. The experimentation and misuse of drugs provides a very graphic example, it seems to me, of why the Neptunian energy is necessarily "veiled" and how a beautiful and subtle energy can have a constructive effect on one level and a destructive effect on another. It is interesting that part of Neptune's work and influence has to do with revealing to us the unreality of the world of shadowy appearances. The seers are often accused of being "unreal" or in "outer space", when, in fact, they see where others do not. Yet a distortion of the Neptunian energy does, indeed, make the accusation a true one. One could say that a distorted or premature use of Neptune brings about the illusion of stepping back from the world of appearances and seeing truly. The irony appears to be: That which can perceive Reality and expose the sublest veil of illusion can also be the greatest illusion creator. It must be remembered, however, that it is not Neptune but self-centered personality (Sun) that causes distortion. ✔

Summary of Neptune Indicators. Below is a summary of qualities and characteristics identifying the Neptune influence:

Sensitivity to and revealing nature of soul.
Bridging towards the God-Man.

Is related primarily to consciousness-quality unfoldment
rather than form-appearance manifestation.
Reveals Heart of the Sun (the real Sun).
Divine contemplations, "view of the upper world."
Development of mystic sense.
Intuitive perception.
Ability to differentiate the real from the unreal.
Idealistic (archetypal) perception.
Envisioning the Plan.
The Crucified Christ.
Purified love nature.
Sublime vibrations requiring refined vehicles.

Negative Influences, Difficulties, Misuse of Energy:
Tendency to "remain above."
Tendency to negate the form, rather than labor to redeem
the form.
Extreme sensitivity.
Enthrallment of the fleshy senses.
Use of and reliance on drugs.
Mystic imperception, mental-emotional fogs, miasmas,
illusions.

Jumping Mouse. In the book *Seven Arrows* Hyemeyohsts Storm tells a symbolic tale of a mouse, which
may be helpful in understanding the Neptunian influence or developmental stage. The Mouse, the story begins, was very *busy,* as mice tend to be. "But once in a
while he would hear an odd *sound.* He would lift his
head, squinting hard to see, his whiskers wiggling in
the *air,* and he would *wonder.*" He would ask the other
mice if they too could hear the odd sound, the "roaring
in your ears," but none of the other mice could. One
day he set off in the *direction* of the roaring. On the
way he met brother Racoon who *knew* what the roar-

ing was and *led* the mouse to the *source* of the sound, which was the River. This was new territory for Mouse, so he was afraid, but he reasoned: After I clarify what this thing is all about, I shall be able to "return to my work and possibly this thing may aid me in all my *busy examining and collecting.*" All his mouse friends had told him that what he thought he heard "was nothing." But now, he thought, he could ask Racoon "to return with me and I will have proof."

Mouse followed Racoon to the River. The River was huge, breathtaking and powerful. Racoon introduced Mouse to Frog, and Frog showed Mouse another step along the path. "Would you like to have some medicine power? . . . Then crouch as low as you can, and then jump as high as you are able! You will have your medicine." Jumping as high as he could, and looking out as far as he was able, he saw the "Sacred Mountains." He landed, however, in the River, which frightened him.

Mouse scurried back to his people. He tried to explain to them something about his extraordinary experience with the River and the Sacred Mountains. No one, however, would listen to him. Since he was still wet from the River, and since it had not rained and there were no puddles, the other mice were "afraid of him. They believed he had been spat from the mouth of another animal that had tried to eat him." If he was not food for the animal, they reasoned, then he must be poison. Mouse managed to live with his people again, but "he could not forget his vision of the Sacred Mountains."

One day Mouse set off in search of the Sacred Mountains. He met an Old Mouse, who knew of the River but not of the Mountains. He met a Great Buffalo, who was dying and could only be cured by the "eye of a mouse." Mouse had never encountered such a Great Being before. "One of my tiny eyes. . . . He will die if I do not give him my eye. He is too great a being to let die." Buffalo responded: "You have given me life so that I may give-away to the people. I will be your Brother forever", and he helped Mouse reach the foot of the Sacred Mountains.

On the way up the Mountain he met Gray Wolf, who had lost the memory of who he was. Without being asked, and though it made him blind (and after much inner struggle), Mouse healed the Wolf with his other eye. Brother Wolf, then, took him up the Mountain to the edge of a Mountain "Medicine Lake" and described the scene to him. At this spot Mouse stood without stirring, bracing himself for possible death beneath the claws of an eagle. "And the Eagle hit! Mouse went to sleep. Then he woke up. The surprise of being alive was great, but now he could see. Everything was blurry, but the colors were beautiful." He heard a voice telling him to "crouch down as low as you can and jump as high as you can. . . . Do not be afraid. Hang on to the wind and trust." Mouse did this and then realized he could fly. He had been transformed into an Eagle (*Seven Arrows,* excerpts from pages 68 to 85).

In Socrates's cave analogy, we find a condition of loosening oneself from the chains of appearances and emerging out of the cave-shadow world into the true light. Upon returning to the fettered ones, the person does not do too well in distinguishing the shadows. In Storm's mouse analogy, we find a tuning to a "roaring," a sound. In both cases—light and sound—we are talking about an inner ear and an inner eye, or a sensing of aspects of life to which people for a long time are "blind" and "deaf." Master Morya writes: "Nothing can transmit an understanding of the Invisible World save the very sensation of it. Nothing can help the heart if it does not desire to surrender itself to this feeling and sensation" (*Heart,* para. 298). Neptune helps us to sense and attune to the invisible, though densely populated, higher worlds.

Mouse sees the River, which designates perhaps the Subtle World, the soul, the second or sentient or consciousness aspect, and the intuition. Mouse glimpses a higher world still, the Sacred Mountains, which, as the highest, the summit, refers to the will, the spiritual will, the first aspect, the Fiery World and esoteric Uranus. The spiritual will and esoteric Uranus touch the physical world and magically transfigure it. We have, then, once again our three conditions:

1. Ordinary life, the "mice."	Exoteric rulers, limitations of the ordinary senses.
2. The aspirant "mouse, jumping mouse" in search of the soul.	Esoteric Neptune, mysticism, esoteric rulers, soul contact, the vision, the greater life that dwarfs the lesser life, the intuitive sense.
3. The transfigured "mouse," the "Eagle."	The sacrificial will, Esoteric Uranus, hierarchical planetary rulers, the Plan, transfiguring the physical condition.

Mouse meets various people or entities along the way. "Racoon" guides him to the River. Mouse begins to sense "something" and begins to search for "something"—and the guide readily appears. Racoons are

clever and independent creatures. The next guide is
"Frog", in this case the one who lives both "above and
within the River . . . the Keeper of the Water." Frog enables him to envision a still higher dimension. Contact
with the soul enables Mouse (who is renamed "Jumping
Mouse" by Frog) to "see" something of that which is
above the soul.

Jumping Mouse, the aspirant endeavoring to tread
the spiritual Path, wants to share his experience and vision with his fellow mice, but they are sceptical. As suggested also in Socrates's cave analogy, his life could be in
danger. His visions, his spiritual experiences, are a threat
to the established order, so they theorize that he may be
"poisonous." Mouse at this point does not have the *power*
to alter conditions in the shadow-world-effects in any significant way. He has the *sensitivity* to attune to the Subtle
Worlds. What is he to do? He cannot simply forget the
vision and assume the activities of "mice." He sets out in
quest of the Sacred Mountains.

During the next stage of his inner journey he meets
three guides. The first is an Old Mouse who knows of the
River but is doubtful of the Mountains. He teaches Mouse
a few things, but Mouse must go beyond the limitations
of the most advanced of his own kind—no easy task. The
next two guides are Beings that he has never seen before.
It is most interesting that in a sense the manifesting life
of these Beings depends upon Mouse. He can "heal"
Them or restore Them to wholeness, to completion, to a
full circulation of Their energies. In other words, some of
the Great Ones must work through man. All creation
waits for man to grow up and grow out of his self-
centeredness. Little "Mouse" plays a significant role in
the divine scheme of things. He can help those great and
powerful Beings Who are far more evolved than himself.
He must, however, "hear" Them. He must figure out

what is required of him. He must understand something of Their work and how he can aid and participate in it. Great and powerful as these Beings are, there is no coercion. Mouse is free to help them or not. In aiding Them, however, he is faced not with reward or remuneration but personal sacrifice. He has to give something up— something not peripheral but vital.

Again, we see the role of the Neptunian energy in the sensing of the inner path, the attunement to subtle and spiritual Beings, the dedication to the path towards the Sacred Mountains, and the sacrifice required. As he moves further up the Sacred Mountains, something of the esoteric Uranian influence can be detected. Mouse sacrifices his only remaining eye. This suggests complete sacrifice for the benefit of the greater Life. As an individual and personal life, he is helpless. That is to say, he must rely completely on the inner Life, since outwardly he is without vision. He must then stand in spiritual being. He must be attuned to and focussed in the causal worlds. There is a shift here. As he sacrificed his one "eye" to the Buffalo, he had, one might say, an eye in both worlds. When both "eyes" were gone, his inward alignment became total and his entire life depended upon it. He had no personal outer life. At this point a transfiguration occurred. His energy body dramatically changed and a "new birth" came about. Rather than a sensing-intuiting-envisioning Neptunian factor, we are dealing at this point with a will-physical alignment, a dense-body revitalization and transfiguration factor—which in all probability tells us something about esoteric Uranus. In summary of the Neptunian factors in the "jumping mouse" tale, we have the following:

Sensing of the Inner Sound, the "Sound" of the Flow of Energy of the Subtle World, the world of qualitative ener-

gies that conditions the world of appearances.
Finding one's way to the River, the Divine Flow.
The need to "jump", or have high aspirations, to strive.
Finding the right and true guides along the way.
Accepting the loneliness of the Path.
Dealing with the problems of extreme sensitivity.
Recognizing how one can help or be of service to the Great
    Inner Beings, how one can let the Great Inner Beings work
    through one.
Dedication to the Spiritual Path.
Personal sacrifice in order to develop the spiritual
    alignment—a purification process, a changing of the
    energy cells.

Humble People Make Discoveries. In the *Bible* it is
recorded that Jesus said to His disciples: "Blessed are
the meek: for they shall inherit the earth" (Matthew
5:5). "Meek" has become associated with weakness,
with being soft and pliant. Is it possible that God is
going to co-create with or delegate administrative responsibility to the weak? Surely, strength is one of the
vital qualities necessary for "inheriting" the earth
and being responsible for the evolutionary development of the sub-kingdoms in nature.

Perhaps the word "humble" with its contemporary connotations might come closer to the intended
meaning of "meek." A key connotation of humbleness
is that it is not self-assertive and not self-exaltative. It
is the antithesis of being proud. But why not be proud?
Why not be self-assertive? If a person has certain abilities that are superior to those of his fellowmen, why
should he not be proud of them? Why should he humble himself and assume a lowly position? And how
does strength fit into this? And one might ask, how

does fear fit into this? And one might ask also, what does it matter if one is humble or not? And why single out meekness, meaning humility, as the particular quality that will result in inheriting the earth?

It seems to me that there are two crucial factors in the attitude of humbleness. First of all, there is the *inner* recognition of one's small yet significant *relationship* with the Cosmic, the Infinite. Secondly, there is the *outer activity* of service to one's fellowman and to all beings. Recognition of the inner relationship with the Infinite has to do with some experience of the hierarchical order of things, of the fact that we are all energy bodies related through strands of light, and that we are in fact "points of light within the Greater Light." This experience is *humbling* because our individual place in the Cosmos is relatively small and the work is immense. It is also humbling (and terrifying) in that our recognition of the reality of our cosmic relationship reveals the irreality of the personal, self-centered outlook with its attendant illusions. The outer activity of service necessarily follows, for recognition of the fact of the inner, lighted, hierarchical relationship, results also in the recognition of the fact of brotherhood. We are inescapably here to help each other work free of the illusion of separation and self-centeredness.

Once again we can see the Neptunian influence facilitating a recognition of the inner relationships and the spiritual facts. We can also see that pride and self-assertiveness are indicative of the developmental stage during which the Sun veils Neptune.

Humble people, then, one could say, make discoveries. Pride indicates self-centeredness, which blocks the intuitive interplay and which veils mystic Neptune. Humility accompanies the recognition of the Higher Kingdoms and the Inner Rulers. Humility—or a recognition of one's true place in the grand scheme of things—is necessary in order to be entrusted with the higher knowledge and the new directions.

The Three Veiled Planets and the Three Crosses.
The Crosses—Mutable, Fixed, Cardinal—can be viewed "outwardly" as different types of energy functioning at the same level, as is the case in orthodox, exoteric astrology. In esoteric astrology, however, they are considered "inwardly" or as energies that manifest at different levels. D. K. makes reference to this in his book *Esoteric Astrology.* In this sense, personalities, regardless of planetary placement in the horoscope, are primarily functioning on the level of the Mutable Cross, souls on the Fixed Cross, and initiates on the Cardinal Cross. Consider the following reference:

1. Upon the *Mutable Cross,* it is the physical Sun and its influences which affect the man, stimulate the bodily cells and sustain the form nature, affecting the centers below the diaphragm.
2. Upon the *Fixed Cross,* it is the "heart of the Sun" which is called into activity and which pours its energies through Neptune upon man. These stimulate and affect the heart, the throat and the ajna centers.
3. Upon the *Cardinal Cross,* it is the central, spiritual Sun which is called into play, and Uranus is then the distributing agency and the head center becomes the center in the initiate's body through which direction and control come. (Bailey, 1951, p. 297).

We have then:

1. Physical Sun . .Mutable Cross . . . . .base of spine,
                                            solar plexus,
                                            sacral centers.
2. Heart of Sun . .Fixed Cross. . . .Neptune . .Heart, throat
                                            and ajna
                                            centers
3. Central,
   Spiritual Sun. .Cardinal Cross .Uranus . . .head center.

In considering that special function of Vulcan, which has to do with the early use of the will in order to direction one towards the higher centers, and in considering the rays involved, we have the following set of correspondences:

3. Uranus. . . . . . .Ray 7 . . . . .1. . . . . . .Cardinal
2. Neptune. . . . . .Ray 6 . . . . .2. . . . . . .Fixed
3. Vulcan . . . . . . .Ray 1 . . . . .3. . . . . . .Mutable

It should be clear at this point that there is something third ray about Vulcan's first ray energy. Also, there is something very second ray about Neptune's sixth ray energy. And there is something first ray about Uranus's seventh ray energy. The one, two, three ray level is actually the obvious factor. In designating the veiled planets, D. K. has given us an additional clue in terms of the energy required during the higher stages.

Imbued with the Group Idea. From a slightly different angle, the same level factor can be considered, which may shed additional light on the subtle and esoteric matter. "I would remind you that the Moon is usually 'veiling' or 'hiding' some planet and of these there are three which the Moon may be veiling. Here the intuition of the astrologer and of the esoteric student must be called out. These planets are Vulcan, Neptune or Uranus. These three create and influence certain aspects of the Mother principle, which nourish and feed the life of the inner divine reality until the time comes when the Christ child is brought to birth. They determine or condition the physical, astral and mental natures, thus creating the personality. They form a triangle of immense creative potency. . . . The point which I am here making is that through the influence of Mercury and Neptune the group consciousness of the individual is developed, so that through the tests in Scorpio and the experience in Aquarius the disciple emerges *on the physical plane* into the position of world server; all world servers are decentralized workers and are governed by the need and the reaction of the mass or group. That is one of the reasons why, when in training, disciples are absorbed into a Master's group which is integrally a collection of individuals who are imbued with the group idea and are learning increasingly to react to it. In this world period and in a peculiar manner, as far as the race (Aryan) to which the Western world belongs, Neptune is known esoterically as the Initiator. In certain ancient formulas, the great Teacher of the West and the present world Initiator, Christ, is spoken of as Neptune, Who rules the oceans, Whose trident and astrological symbol signifies the Trinity in manifestation and Who is the ruler of the Piscean Age. The formula runs as follows, speaking esoterically: ' . . . the fish goddesses who have leapt from earth (Virgo) to water (Pisces) unitedly give birth to the Fish God (Christ) who introduces the water of life into the ocean of substance and thus brings light to the world. Thus does Neptune work.' This is, however, a great mystery, revealed only at the time of the second initiation in which the control of the fluidic astral plane is demonstrated" (Bailey 1951, pp. 219–220).

The following three diagrams may help to illustrate the particular lines of emphasis, the planes of manifestation, and the particular vehicles of expression in respect to the Vulcan, Neptunian, and Uranian levels of consciousness under discussion. These diagrams have been adapted from *Treatise on Cosmic Fire* by Alice Bailey (Chart VIII, The Egoic Lotus and the Centers). Each of the seven planes are divided into seven sub-planes; we have only indicated this in the diagrams in the case of the physical plane. The mental plane is divided into higher abstract mind (arupa) and the lower mind or intellect (rupa). The Egoic Lotus is the soul body and is on the abstract sub-planes of the mental plane. All seven planes represented are the seven sub-planes of the cosmic physical plane. In other words, our astral plane is the cosmic liquid sub-plane, our mental plane is the cosmic gaseous sub-plane.

Diagram I is suggestive of the Vulcan alignment. Vulcan is related to the energy transference from the etheric sacral center to the throat center, with its higher correspondences on the astral and mental planes. The knowledge petals of the egoic (soul) lotus are generally the first to unfold. They constitute the activity aspect (the third aspect, the throat) in the triplicity of will, love and light (knowledge). This aspect of the soul is related to the higher abstract mind and activity aspect of the monad. With Vulcan at this level, we are talking about the use of the will, first ray, in a re-directioning of activity to a higher mode of creativity. There is the emergence "from darkness into light."

Plane of Adi			Logoic Plane

Monadic Plane — Will — Wisdom — Active Intelligence

| Atmic-Nirvanic Plane | Atmic Permanent Atom | Spiritual Will |

| Buddhic Plane | Buddhic Permanent Atom | Intuition |

| Mental Plane | Knowledge Petals of Egoic Lotus | Manasic Permanent Atom | Higher Mind |

S.C. — Lower Mind, Intellect

| Astral Plane | Throat Center | Emotion Sentient Plane |

S.C.

Physical Plane		First Ether
		Second Ether
	Throat Center	Third Ether
		Fourth Ether
	Sacral Center	Gas
		Liquid
		Solid

DIAGRAM I - VULCAN ALIGNMENT

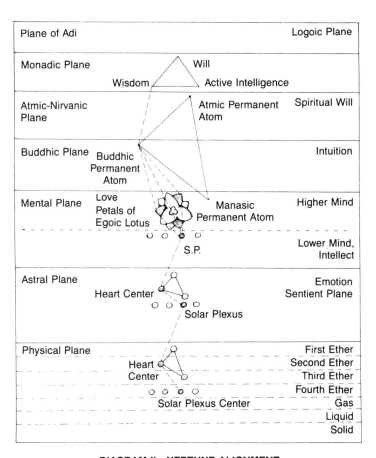

DIAGRAM II - NEPTUNE ALIGNMENT

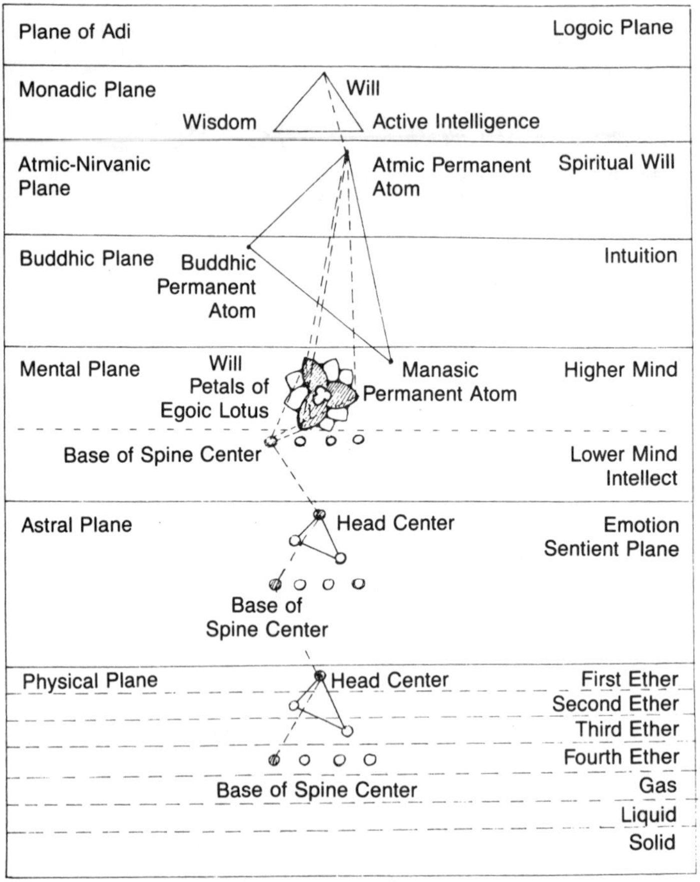

Plane of Adi	Logoic Plane

Monadic Plane — Will

Wisdom — Active Intelligence

Atmic-Nirvanic Plane — Atmic Permanent Atom — Spiritual Will

Buddhic Plane — Buddhic Permanent Atom — Intuition

Mental Plane — Will Petals of Egoic Lotus — Manasic Permanent Atom — Higher Mind

Base of Spine Center — Lower Mind Intellect

Astral Plane — Head Center — Emotion Sentient Plane

Base of Spine Center

Physical Plane — Head Center — First Ether

Second Ether

Third Ether

Fourth Ether

Base of Spine Center — Gas

Liquid

Solid

DIAGRAM III - URANUS ALIGNMENT

Diagram II is suggestive of the Neptune alignment. There is an energy transference from the solar plexus to the heart. In the case of Vulcan, the physical body is involved. In the case of Neptune, the astral body receives the primary attention. The love petals of the soul (egoic lotus) are related to the buddhic aspect (intuition) of the spiritual triad. The personality emerges from the "unreal to the real."

Diagram III is suggestive of the Uranus alignment. The alignment includes the base of the spine and head (crown) center, the mental body, the will aspect of the soul, atma aspect of the spiritual triad and will aspect of the monad. For the initiate there is the emergence from "death to immortality."

It should become increasingly clear that esoteric astrology-psychology deals with inner dimensions (inclusive of soul and planes higher), whereas exoteric astrology-psychology deals with the relatively outer activities of personality. The outer factors are analogous of the inner. The crosses are an example. Outwardly or exoterically, the three crosses—Cardinal, Fixed, Mutable—all come into play. But as they symbolize the inner dimensions, then personality is always on the Mutable Cross, soul on the Fixed Cross (the disciple), and spiritual triad on the Cardinal (the initiate). The horizontal, visible world is a map and symbol of the vertical, invisible worlds. We have a similar situation in the case of Vulcan, Neptune and Uranus. These planets can be viewed outwardly as they affect personality. Or they can be viewed inwardly as they designate the three major levels of consciousness under discussion.

If we consider again the three stages in the following terms,

1. Spirit . . . . .synthesis . . . . . .god-consciousness
2. Soul . . . . .unity. . . . . .group consciousness
3. Personality. . . . .integration. . . . .self-consciousness
we see that the second level of Neptune has much to do with
being "imbued with the group idea." There is then a transition from personality individualism, competitiveness, self-
centeredness and aggressiveness to the true inclusiveness
and brotherhood of the soul. D. K. writes: "Remember that
the evocation of the rhythm of the heart center is demonstrated in the early stages by an increasing understanding
of individuals and a growing awareness of group problems.
Later it produces definite group consciousness and awareness of the Plan" (Bailey, 1944, p. 296). The second heart-
consciousness-soul stage is itself here divided into three
stages:

Spirit. . . . .
        ┌ . . . .awareness of the Plan, relating soul to will and
        │   spirit.
Soul   │ . . . .definite group consciousness.
        └ . . . .increasing understanding of individuals, group
               problems, as one decentralizes from personality.
Personality . . . .

What is developed then here through Neptune is not
group politics, group organization, group manipula-
tion and group control, but group *understanding,*
group *consciousness,* that is, being of one heart and
mind. This must have to do with the development of
that extremely rare thing of a true brotherhood.

**William James's "Varieties of Religious Experi-
ence."** At the turn of the century William James gave
a series of lectures at the University of Edinburgh
that were compiled into his well-known book: *The Varieties of Religious Experience.* James's approach to

the study is an empirical one. His book is said to be a classic in three areas: in philosophical, scientific and religious thought. Many things that James discussed are helpful in our own effort to understand the Neptunian energy.

We have implied three stages of the Neptune experience. The first stage has to do with the growing dissatisfaction with the visible world or with the world of appearances. At the same time there is a subtle and vague attraction to something higher, something more real. This first stage could be called "the sensing of the distant roaring of the River." The second stage has to do with the elevating mystic experience, the communion with the invisible world. Here the reality of the unseen alters the life's direction and becomes henceforth a major conditioning factor in the person's life. This stage could be called "the experience of the River and the glimpse of the Magic Mountain." This second stage seems to be the heart of the Neptune experience. The third stage has to do with the question of how to relate the vision to the shadowy world—a world that basically rejects the call to the selflessness of the higher worlds. The third stage leads to the acquisition of additional energies in order to make dynamically effective the Neptunian insights. The third stage leads to the ascension of the mountain. It is also a stage in which cooperation with higher Beings, such as the Masters, and cooperation with the Plan is required.

During the first stage there is a turning away from the material or conventional world. James describes asceticism as symbolizing "the belief that there is an element of real wrongness in this world, which . . . must be squarely met and overcome by an appeal to the soul's heroic resources, and neutralized and cleansed away by suffering" (James, p. 287). In a certain sense, the aspirant at one stage is forced to make a choice: "Shall the seen or the unseen world be our chief sphere of adaptation?" (James, p. 205). One could say that the candidate for Neptune at the esoteric level is offended (not necessarily in a personal sense but in a philosophical sense) with the "wrongness" and apparent injustice in the world. He is offended to the degree that if his deeper questions as to the meaning of it all are not answerable, he is not sure if life—as a superficial activity for temporary survival—is worth living. One might say that the earnestness of the aspirant's inner appeal is evidenced through a period-process of self-denial and renunciation, as far as the material and personality trappings of the world of appearances is concerned. In the process he or she is trying to see behind the veil or destroy something of that veil of illusory self-centeredness.

The first stage, then, is a decision making, a new direction, a new commitment leading to new activities. The second stage is the development of the Neptunian energy and the consciousness. William James lists certain attitudes and realizations that identify or accompany the mystical saintly and profoundly religious experience.

1. First of all there is the realization that the visible is *not* all there is but is in fact "part of a more spiritual universe from which it draws its chief significance."
2. That "union or harmonious relation with that higher universe is our true end."
3. There is also the realization that "inner communion with the spirit . . . is a process wherein work is

really done, and spiritual energy flows in and produces effects, psychological or material, within the
phenomenal world."
4. The mystic realizations may also be accompanied
by a "new zest which ... takes the form either of
lyrical enchantment or of appeal to earnestness and
heroism." There may also be a sense of "safety" and
"peace" and a "preponderance of loving affection"
(James, p. 377).

There is also the "feeling of being in a wider life than
that of this world's selfish little interests; and a con-
viction, not merely intellectual but as it were sensible,
of the existence of an Ideal Power...." There is a
"willing self-surrender" to the control of the "Ideal
Power." This is often accompanied by an "immense
elation and freedom, as the outlines of the confining
selfhood melt down." There is an "increase of purity",
and in place of fears and anxieties one experiences
"equanimity" (James, p. 220).

A point that William James makes in several
places in the book is that something other than intellect and reason is at work in the attunement with the
higher worlds. The mystic state includes "insights
into depths of truth unplumbed by the discursive
intellect." Mystical states "break down the authority
of rationalistic consciousness, based upon the understanding and the senses alone.... They open up the
possibility of other sources of truth." Reason and logic
are secondary to "our inarticulate feelings of
reality.... The unreasoned and immediate assurance
is the deep thing in us," whereas the "reasoned argu-
ment" has to do with "a phony translation into formulas" (James, pp. 300, 331, 74). The lower concrete
mind or intellect is primarily an instrument of the

personality. At a certain stage of development the personality has difficulty conceiving of anything higher. Neptune is instrumental, it seems to me, in developing the higher and subtler vehicles of consciousness, which include the soul, the higher abstract mind and the intuition. We find the statement in *Treatise on Cosmic Fire* that Neptune "has a vital relation to the sixth logoic principle, or Buddhi, and therefore the sixth principle of man. No man begins to co-ordinate the buddhic vehicles [intuition] until he comes under Neptunian influence in some life or another" (Bailey, 1925, p. 899).

After acquiring knowledge of the higher worlds in some degree, how does one relate the inner light (the Heart of the Sun) with the shadowy world of appearances (physical Sun as it symbolizes personality). How does the aspirant become the disciple and initiate? How does one who has emerged out of the cave (in Plato's analogy) return to the cave and function in the world of inversion—where the unreal is called real, and the real is called unreal? To quote James: "St. Paul long ago made our ancestors familiar with the idea that every soul is virtually sacred. . . . This belief in the essential sacredness of everyone expresses itself today in all sorts of humane customs and reformatory institutions, and in a growing aversion to the death penalty and to brutality in punishment. The saints, with their extravagance of human tenderness, are the great torch-bearers of this belief, the tip of the wedge, the clearer of the darkness. Like the single drops which sparkle in the sun as they are flung far ahead of the advancing edge of a wave-crest or of a flood, they show the way and are forerunners. The world is not yet with them, so they often seem in the midst of the world's affairs to be preposterous. Yet they are impregnators of the world, vivifiers and animaters of potentialities of goodness which but for them would be forever dormant. It is not possible to be quite as mean as we naturally are, when they have passed before us. One fire kindles another; and without that overtrust in human worth which they show, the rest of us would be in spiritual stagnancy" (James, p. 283-4).

The third stage has to do with presenting the ideas and undertaking the labor that will be termed "preposterous" by those who are limited by the personal perspective. Here are the forerunners who "impregnate" the consciousness of humanity with seeds that will bear fruit many years later. One of the problems is that, indeed, they are often "flung so far ahead" that the bridging work becomes excruciatingly difficult. Again, we see how the mystic is led to become the occultist—esoteric Uranus supersedes esoteric Neptune.

Some of the negative characteristics of the religious experience are also identified by William James. Some "geniuses in the religious line" have "often shown symptoms of nervous instability," have been subject to "abnormal psychical visitations", have had a "discordant inner life", have had "melancholy [depression] during part of their careers", and have been "liable to obsessions and fixed ideas" (James, p. 25). James also makes the interesting points: "Fanaticism is found only where the character is masterful and aggressive. In gentle characters, where devoutness is intense and the intellect feeble, we have an imaginative absorption in the love of God to the exclusion of all practical human interests, which, though innocent enough, is too one-sided to be admirable. A mind too narrow has room but for one kind of affection" (James, p. 273).

Summary. Some Neptune indicators at the three stages are listed below:

Stage I.
—Profound dissatisfaction with the world of appearances.
—Need to undergo an ascetic type of self-denial in order to purify and detach oneself from the outer world.
—Seeking those directions that lead to the worlds that could be called "super-appearance" (instead of "supernatural").
—The aspirant.
Stage II.
—Inner communication with some aspects of the "spiritual universe."
—The unseen becomes "seen" or known.
—The outer world is seen as the world of effects and as being dependent upon the "higher universe."
—The inner attunement is sometimes accompanied by:
    Lyrical enchantment, joy, bliss.
    An appeal to heroism or labors of a higher order.
    A profound sense of love and peace.
    Experience with an Ideal Power.
    Willingness to make sacrifices for the Ideal Power or higher Will.
    Knowledge that is beyond or higher than reason and intellect.
    Intuitive insights.
Stage III.
—Labor to bring about more humane conditions.
—Mystic endeavoring to be occultist.
—Working from perspective of essential sacredness and oneness of all creation.
—Being a forerunner, a torch-bearer, an animator of potentialities of goodness.

Negative Characteristics:
—Abnormal psychic visitations.
—Nervous instability.
—Depression, melancholy.
—Liable to fixed ideas, obsessions.
—Fanatacism.

Going with the Flow. The colloquial expression "going with the flow" and the esoteric phrase "the Divine Circulatory Flow" seem to have value here in terms of attuning to Neptune, "the God of the Waters." The "Flow" implies something that is continuously moving and *changing*, and also something that is *all-pervasive*. There is a *non-intellectual* or supra-intellectual factor here, as the case always is with Neptune. Our movement or change can be calculated to a degree intellectually. But to "go with the Flow" is to take a step of faith, to walk where one is intellectually unsure, to step into a series of events that cannot be predicted on the basis of our knowledge of past events.

If the Flow is all-pervasive, how is it possible that one can remove oneself from the Flow? The phrase "the Divine Circulatory Flow" suggests that there is a continuous and unimpeded energy relationship from the "highest" to the "lowest." Perhaps we can think of this in terms of cosmic-systemic-planetary energies, or in terms of the seven planes of manifestation: the plane of adi or divinity, the monadic plane, atmic plane of spiritual will, buddhic plane of intuition, manasic or mental plane, astral or emotional plane, and the etheric-physical plane. Or we can think of this in terms of the kingdoms in nature: the mineral, vegetable, animal, human, egoic (soul), planetary and solar lives or kingdoms. From our observations of the lower kingdoms and presumably from our sensed and secondhand knowledge of the higher kingdoms, one could say that only the human kingdom (or more particularly, the Atlantean and Aryan Root Races) has the capacity to remove itself from the Divine Circulatory Flow. It might also be helpful to think of this in terms of instinct, to intellect, to intuition. The following tabulation might help clarify:

1.	Instinct	Unconsciously within the Divine Flow.	Animal, childhood, primitive man.
2.	Intellect	Self-centered separation from Divine Flow.	Self-conscious man, exoteric Sun.
3.	Intuition	Conscious cooperation with Flow, leading to unity and synthesis.	Spiritual man, esoteric Neptune.

These are broad and very general stages.

Some myths might shed light on the above. The Adam and Eve myth indicates a removal from an aligned and harmonious state to one of a misuse of knowledge, which removed them (us) from the Divine Flow. The expulsion from the Garden of Eden occurred when the "creative power was abused," when the "divine gift was desecrated," and the life essence was wasted "for no purpose except bestial personal gratification" (*Secret Doctrine*, vol. 3, p. 409).

The myth of Prometheus may help us understand man's temporary removal from the Divine Circulatory Flow. Prometheus defied Zeus, took a glowing charcoal from Mount Olympus, concealed it in a long fennel-stalk, and brought fire to mankind. For this "theft" Prometheus was chained to a pillar in the Caucasian Mountains—his liver being consumed by a vulture during the day and growing whole again at night. The "fire" that Prometheus brought to mankind resulted in many benefits. It proved to be the teacher of all kinds of crafts, enabled man to understand the movement of the stars and the art of using numbers. Through fire man was able to emerge out of a cave existence and control the wild beasts. By its means man learned architecture, navigation, medicine, metallurgy and other useful arts.

Prometheus (meaning "forethought") also gathered all the evil things of the world—Sickness, Labor, Insanity, Vice, Passion, Old Age, etc.—and put them into a large pot. He sealed the pot and gave it to his brother, Epimetheus (meaning "afterthought"), for safe keeping. Epimetheus allowed Pandora access to the sealed pot, which resulted in the release of the various ills onto mankind. Hope, however, was also included amongst the diverse ills, and Hope prevented a general suicide.

The Secret Doctrine interprets the myth in the following way: "The Host that incarnated in a portion of humanity, though led to it by Karma or Nemesis, preferred free will to passive slavery, intellectual self-conscious pain and even torture . . . to inane, imbecile, instinctual beatitude. Knowing such an incarnation was premature and not in the programme of Nature, the Heavenly Host, 'Prometheus', still sacrificed itself to benefit thereby, at least, one portion of mankind. But while saving man from mental darkness, they inflicted upon him the tortures of the self-consciousness of his responsibility—the result of his free will—besides every ill to which mortal man and flesh are heir" (*Secret Doctrine,* v.3, p. 419). In a sense, Prometheus is "the representation of humanity—active, industrious, which aims at equalling divine Powers" (v.

4, p. 94). He is a "symbol and a personification of the whole of mankind in relation to an event which occurred during its childhood, ... The 'Baptism of Fire'—which is a mystery within the great Promethean Mystery. ... By reason of the extraordinary growth of human intellect and the development in our age of the fifth principle (Manas) in man, its rapid progress has paralyzed spiritual perceptions. It is at the expense of wisdom that intellect generally lives, and mankind is quite unprepared in its present condition to comprehend the awful drama of human disobedience to the laws of Nature and the subsequent Fall, as a result" (*S.D.*, v. 5,p. 323).

Once again, then, generally speaking, we seem to have indicated three major stages:

STAGE ONE:

    This, evidently, is a pre-intellectual stage, one of "instinctual beautitude", of racial childhood, and of "passive slavery." It is described elsewhere in the *Secret Doctrine* as living under a "protecting shadow ... without desire as without fear ... the blessed peace of childhood's dreams" (v. 4, p. 89). Prometheus, however, brought fire to mankind (which is to say that a new psychic energy was made available to mankind) and transformed "the most perfect of animals on Earth into a potential God", allowing them to proceed *consciously* on the path of Spiritual Evolution" (v. 3, p. 246). This, then, brought mankind to:

STAGE TWO:

    This stage can evidently be divided into its positive and negative aspects.

    Stage Two, Positive: Free will, development of intellectual self-consciousness, developing responsibility, active, intelligent, ambitious, and aspiring to divine Powers. Intellectual powers developed the useful arts, sciences, business, architecture, etc., which were of much benefit to mankind.

Stage Two, Negative: Egotistical and selfish, a slave to the earthly passions, "feeling the vulture of doubt and full consciousness gnawing at its heart" (v. 3, p. 247), "chronic animalism and sensuality," and intellect developed at the expense of wisdom.

STAGE THREE.

This stage has to do with a conscious obedience and forethought, rather than disobedience and afterthought—obedience to the laws of Nature and God's Will. It also has to do with wisdom, spiritual perception, intuition and altruism, for "the divine Titan [Prometheus] is moved by altruism, but the mortal man by selfishness and egoism in every instance" (S. D., v. 3, p. 420).

Prometheus endowed man with that "wisdom which ministers to physical well-being," but lower mind or kama-manas (desire-mind) tends to dominate man. "Instead of an 'untainted mind, heaven's first gift,' there was created the eternal vulture of ever unsatisfied desire, of regret and despair, coupled with the dreamlike feebleness that fetters the blind race of mortals, until the day when Prometheus is released by his heaven-appointed deliver, Herakles" (S. D., v. 3, pp. 410, 411). "Prometheus—the divine aspect of Manas merging and aspiring to Buddhi—was the divine Soul." This is contrasted to the "lowest aspect of human physical intelligence—Manas wedded to Kama" (Secret Doctrine, v. 3, p. 417). See Diagram IV.

Intellect, self-consciousness and kama-manas (desire-mind) have much to do with temporarily removing mankind from the Divine Flow. Desire-mind and intellectual self-centeredness have much to do

PROMETHEUS BOUND   PROMETHEUS UNBOUND

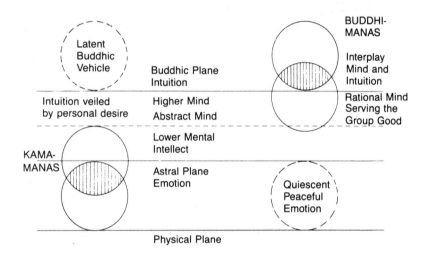

(Shaded area indicates focus of consciousness)

KAMA-MANAS   BUDDHI-MANAS

DESIRE MIND   INTUITIVE MIND

Disobedient to Laws of Nature   Co-creates with Nature

Selfish, egotistical   Altruistic

Unsatisfied desire and   Untainted spiritual perception
intellectual materialism

DIAGRAM IV

with releasing the pain of greed, passion, vice, despair, disease, etc., onto the human family. As the Buddha said, the cessation of suffering is related to the cessation of desire. Since kama-manas is the dominant focal point of consciousness of humanity today, one does not realize how collectively disturbed or "insane", that is, unsound, unhealthy, or unwhole, humanity is. It is as if pain (physical, emotional and mental) has become the norm, whereas inspiration, joy, right livelihood and right relationship could be our daily bread.

One of the interesting points to realize here is that collectively a family, a group of people, a system or organization of people, a nation, a race, or humanity as a whole can remove itself from the Divine Flow through selfishness, egoism, personal desire-mind, a misuse of the intellect, etc. In this regard, consider the following statements by Roger Walsh. As part of Roger Walsh's post-doctoral training in psychiatry, he had to undergo psychotherapy himself. His therapist worked with him in such a way as to develop "heightened sensitivity to, and appreciation of one's inner experience and subjective world. . . . The range and richness of this internal universe amazed and continues to amaze me. . . . I came to think of this world as a very attractive, pleasant source of positive information." Up to this point, he had been climbing the ladder of success in the shadowy world of established outer systems. Here, however, was something dynamically "new", profound and also questionable in terms of the established norms. He realized that "some of the traditional psychiatric models and assumptions tended to misinterpret and pathologize certain nonpathological states and experiences which occurred with heightened sensitivity to experience. Indeed, I began to suspect that a significant number of our traditional cultural values and assumptions about our psychological nature were distressingly incorrect, illusory and productive of unnecessary suffering." He thought that he had been an intelligent and rational human being preoccupied with "cognition, planning and problem solving." Now, however, he saw that this so-called cognition had been made up primarily of a "frantic torrent of forceful, demanding, loud and often unrelated thoughts and fantasies." He considers this kind of mental activity a virtual "prison . . . of which we remain largely unaware unless we undertake intensive perception training" (Roger Walsh, "Things Are Not As They Seemed", in *Awakening the Heart,* ed. John Welwood).

The Sun veils Neptune. The selfishness, the egotism of the self-centered personality veils the Neptunian path of heightened sensitivity to the altruistic, group consciousness of the soul—the Heart of the Sun. The path of selfishness, which rules and dominates in society today, is permeated with assumptions that are "distressingly incorrect and illusory." Another phrase that Roger Walsh uses to describe our contemporary condition is: "We effectively share a mass cultural hypnosis." Perhaps this is a modern way of saying that we are preoccupied with shadows on a cave wall.

Another contemporary psychologist, Erich Fromm, sees an underlying problem of man as being one of "alienation" in contrast to a needed sense of "well-being." Unlike the animal that instinctually adapts to the environment, man has "awareness of himself as a separate entity," which makes him "feel unbearably alone, lost, powerless." The question then is: "How can we find union within ourselves, with our fellowman, with nature?" Fromm sees two basic answers: (1) "regressing to the state of unity which existed before awareness ever arose, that is, before man was born", or (2) becoming "fully born", developing "one's awareness, one's reason, one's capacity to love, to such a point that one transcends one's own egocentric involvement, and arrives at a new harmony, at a new oneness with the world." Once again we see a recognition (implied or stated) of an earlier state of unity (animal, instinctual, childhood or pre-birth)—a unity that lacks full consciousness, a unity that is automatic and therefore lacks co-creative powers. The unconscious unity is followed by self-consciousness and individualization—the agony of separation and alienation. Within the state of separation is the hope, the longing and the quest for a transcendent unity and oneness with the world. Erich Fromm states that "once man is torn away from the prehuman, paradisiacal unity with nature, he can never go back to where he came from; two angels with fiery swords block his return." The reference here is obviously to the biblical myth of Adam and Eve: The Lord God "drove out the man; and he placed at the east of the garden of Eden Cherubims, and a flaming sword which turned every way, to keep the way of the tree of life" (*Genesis,* chapt. 3, verse, 24). The tree of knowledge may be related to the fire that Prometheus brought to mankind. The misuse of knowledge (of intellect, of the fire of mind) resulted in a removal from the garden of Eden. Man's own thinking erodes the paradisiacal unity of childhood. The development of intellect removes primitive man from his instinctual harmony with nature. But the fruit of the tree of knowledge, the apple, was to be eaten. The forbidding of dangerous things is often sim-

ply a protection extended to the unready. When suffi-
cient strength is developed (physical-emotional) then
knowledge (mental-intellectual) will be gained. With
knowledge, however, comes the responsibility of sal-
vaging the ill effects of misused knowledge. Similarly,
we *will* partake of the tree of life. We *will* return to the
paradisiacal garden but, due to the "flaming sword
which turned every way", not prematurely. A mistake
with the energy of the tree of life must be far far more
serious (to make a mild understatement) than a mistake with the energy of the tree of knowledge (albeit,
only hope prevents a general suicide).

According to Fromm, man "puts his thought images into things" which distorts his perception of reality. "It is the thought image, the *distorting veil,* that
creates his passions, his anxieties" (my italics). "Eventually, the repressed man, instead of experiencing
things and persons, experiences by *cerebration.* He is
under the illusion of being in touch with the *world,*
while he is only in touch with *words."* Fromm goes on
to say that "to enlarge consciousness means to wake
up, *to lift a veil, to leave the cave,* to bring light into
darkness" (my italics).

Another interesting point that Fromm makes is
the following: "Well-being is the state of having arrived at the full development of reason: reason not in
the sense of merely intellectual judgement, but in that
grasping truth by 'letting things be' (to use Heideg-
ger's term) as they are" (Erich Fromm, "The Nature of
Well-Being" in *Awakening the Heart,* ed. John Welwood, pp. 59–70). This "letting things be" may very
well be related to "going with the Flow." It is evidently
not a negative acquiescence but a detachment from
the interfering, distorting personal "I" consciousness.
It is not a non-thinking passive state but a state in

which reason is developed yet subordinated to something higher. Reason in this sense implements rather than interfers with the Divine Flow. The alignment and attunment has much to do with Neptune and the heart. What one does with the resulting Neptunian insights and revelations depends upon the other developed ray and astrological and chakra energies one has at one's disposal.

Ken Wilber in his book *Up From Eden, A Transpersonal View of Human Evolution* identifies three major developmental stages of human consciousness: Pre-Personal, Personal and Transpersonal. Below are some brief identifiers of these three stages:

Pre-Personal
   primal, instinctual
   undifferentiated
   animal impulses
   Dawn Man
   "dreamy impression in and oneness with the material
      world" (p. 231)
   ignorant of boundaries
   ignorant of time and space
   Eden, personal slumber
   unself-conscious
Personal
   separation, division
   knowledge (intellectual development)
   reflection (self-consciousness)
   reason, logic
   personality
   personal possession
   seeking, grasping, wishing, desiring
   never satisfied (due to seeking unreal substitutes for the
      real)
Transpersonal

death and transcendence of the separate self
transcends life, death, time, space
superconsciousness, saintly, causal
unity, absolute

According to Ken Wilber, the ego, that is personality, "rose up arrogant and aggressive, and . . . began to sever its roots in a fantasy attempt to prove its absolute independence. . . . What we don't realize today is just what the typical self of every previous stage failed likewise to comprehend: *this* [the present stage of personality development] is not the highest and greatest mode of consciousness which can be attained—there lie ahead the realms of superconsciousness, and the pitiful ego, by comparison, is a speck of nothingness. . . . It attempted—and succeeded—in repressing access to both realms, and imagining success, began to remake the cosmos in its own image" (Wilber, p. 182).

The above statement helps us appreciate what Neptune and the transpersonal energies are up against. There seems to be nothing less than a life and death struggle—both within ourselves and outside in the world. Ironically, the transitory personality courts death in its egotism and selfish desires, but does not accept its own death. It attempts to live as if it would never die. The incarnating, transpersonal soul, on the other hand, accepts daily the death of all manifestations, including its own personality and creations, and therefore impersonally courts life.

Summary.

—Going with the Flow is related to the Divine Circulatory Flow and the One Life.

—The Flow encompasses areas and levels of being that are beyond intellectual scrutiny, such as the soul, the intuition, the spiritual will, the future, etc.

—Adam and Eve, and also Prometheus are myths that characterize a human being's tendency to remove him/herself from the harmony of the Divine Flow at a particular stage of racial and individual development.

—On a lesser, non-individualized level the Flow is related to the instinctual beautitude of childhood and primitive man.

—The necessary stages of individuality, personality and intellectual development tend to bring about a separation from the Divine Flow, with its attendant ills, including unsatisfied desire, regret, pain, and a dreamlike feebleness.

—Groups of people (communities, disciplines or fields of work and study, organizations, nations, races, etc.) can remove themselves from the Flow and temporarily share a mass cultural hypnosis.

—Re-alignment with the Flow has much to do with Neptune and the Heart of the Sun. It is related to a profound sense of unity and also to a superconsciousness that transcends the limitations of time-space and personal life-death.

The Heart. In our effort to understand Neptune at the esoteric or soul level, it might be helpful to briefly allude to the book *Heart*, published by the Agni Yoga Society. Master Morya states that "if human psychology were supplemented by a study of the Subtle World, which links the essence of all conditions of existence, our earthly world would then at once change into a distinctly new era. I affirm that the noise of the turmoil has reached unprecedented limits, because the bond between the worlds is completely neglected" (*Heart*, p. 117). The term "Subtle World" is used in contrast with the form world or earthly world and also

in contrast to the higher "Fiery World" or spiritual
will. The Subtle World is related to soul-consciousness
and is beyond "human psychology" that studies primarily the mental-emotional aspects of man. We have
repeatedly drawn attention to Neptune's role of linking the invisible with the visible, the soul with personality, the heart with the form, the inner with the
outer. It is interesting to describe the function of the
heart as "linking the essence of all conditions of existence." The outer form, the periphery, is diverse and
multifaceted. But unity and right relationship come
about when the essence (the inner, heart factor) is recognized. Once again we can say that the heart is a
healing, therefore transforming energy, which when
applied collectively would immediately bring about a
"new era." And again there is the paradox: Neptune
appears impractical as it concerns itself with fantasy
and imagination, yet as it aligns one with the energy
of the Heart of the Sun, it is intensely practical. Another way of saying this is that "without a vision, the
people perish." The labor of correctly envisioning
the next step ahead (which is Neptune's art) is most
essential.

"Humanity has educated itself in coarse forms in
everything, having eschewed refinement and straight-
knowledge. Even the most intrusive signs of the Subtle World are exiled to oblivion" (*Heart,* p. 119).

"If people are trying to perfect even the scientific
apparatuses, then how desirable is the sensitizing of
the human apparatus itself! But without attracting
the help of the heart it is impossible to advance to this
achievement" (*Heart,* p. 52).

"One can think with the brain or with the
heart. . . . Without relieving the brain of work, we are

ready to recognize the heart as a moving power. . . . We must bring the entire world into the sphere of the heart, because the heart is the microcosm of existence. . . . We recall the far-off worlds, but it is the heart, not the brain, that can remember Infinity" (*Heart*, pp. 165– 6).

"Many valuable transmissions will assume an ugly outline, simply because the heart remained neglected. Such a multitude of the best, the subtlest shadings and feelings, will be absent from the forsaken heart. . . . One cannot build up the brain without refinement of the heart. Ancient metaphysics and modern psychology attempt to reach the heart, but how can any subject matter reach the heart when the word *heart* itself is not mentioned? He who does not think of the heart will also fail to improve his consciousness" (*Heart*, p. 209).

"It can be said that for the last century the West has accepted the methods of the brain because they are apparent, although superficial and imperfect, like everything else that necessitates external technique. . . . In order to approach the method of the heart it is necessary to love the world of the heart, or more correctly, to learn to respect all things pertaining to the heart. Many people imagine absolutely no difference between the paths of brain and heart. It is difficult for such 'brain people' to accept the highest worlds. So, too, they cannot picture to themselves the advantages of the Subtle World. . . . To behold flowers of the Subtle World means already to ascend into the Beautiful Sphere. . . . Thus, the heart is not an abstraction, but a bridge to the highest worlds" (*Heart*, pp. 229–30).

The Sun Veils Uranus

Esoteric Astrology. D. K. mentions in *Esoteric Astrology* that the "human being in his eventual recognized group relationships is of more importance than appears in his individual life, which the orthodox horoscope seeks to elucidate. It only determines his little destiny and unimportant fate. Esoteric astrology indicates his group usefulness and the scope of his potential consciousness" (Bailey, 1951, p. 99). It seems to me that our consideration of D. K.'s "veiled" planets—Vulcan, Neptune and Uranus—is one example (of a great many D. K. has given us) of esoteric factors indicating group usefulness. When we consider these three planets "vertically" (levels of consciousness: personality-soul-spirit), then we have to question whether or not the self-centered "orthodox horoscope" is applicable. It becomes, it seems to me, *not* a question of what conditions are beneficial or problematical

to us in a personal way (one's "little destiny"). Rather
it becomes a question of what energies are vitally affecting what "group" condition, and then how can we
intelligently, scientifically, and lovingly facilitate the
right manifestation of those energies for the general
and group good. In this particular case the "group"
conditions has to do with the collective and broad and
comprehensive work of aligning soul and personality
(attuning to higher worlds, the Subtle World), and
then the further work of providing a perfected vehicle
for the dynamic manifestation of the Spiritual Will. It
seems to me that the position of the three planets in
the orthodox horoscope may not necessarily be a good
indicator as to our esoteric accessibility to the energies. From an esoteric point of view, there may be a
need to develop energies (provide an adequate vehicle
for the energies of) Neptune and Uranus, in spite of
house, sign and aspect relationship in the chart. In
this regard, D. K. mentions that exoteric astrology
and the personality horoscope will continue to "prove
its usefulness where the average man is in question,
focussed in his personality life and oriented towards
the material world." D. K. has, however, also "pointed
to the first dim outline of the astrology of the soul and
of the unfolding consciousness of man" (Bailey, 1951,
pp. 497, 498). "Esoteric astrology is concerned with
the soul and not with the form and, therefore, all that
I have to say refers to consciousness, to its expansion,
to its effect upon its vehicles, the form, and—in the
last analysis (as will be later established)—with the
Science of Initiation" (p. 484). Whenever any "dim
outline" is given from hierarchical sources, then it
awaits the human labor of doing something with the
outline—understanding it, elucidating and interpret-

ing it, amplifying and vivifying it with our own experience, stepping it down without distorting it, etc.

Uranus: The Highly Developed Person. In respect to Uranus, once again, it has been suggested that astrologers work when *considering the highly developed man* (Bailey, 1951, p. 13). Basically, what is the Uranian energy and how does it differ from the previous Neptunian stage? Referring to our mythological outline: We find the person liberated from Plato's cave, coming back to the world of shadows and altering it in some significant and dynamic way. In the Indian tale, we see the "mouse", who sacrificingly healed great Beings, becoming transfigured on the mountain top and becoming the initiate, no longer restricted by Saturn. To phrase it another way: "His [the initiate's] will is focused and developed by the Uranian influences and he develops into a leader. He brings about desired changes and produces those conditions which will help the soul of humanity to express itself more freely. . . . The seventh ray is, in the last analysis, the focussed differentiated energy of Ray One as it expresses the will of the first aspect of divinity on earth through the power to relate and bring into objective manifestation— by an act of the will—both spirit and matter" (Bailey, 1951, p. 138).

Comparing this stage with the earlier, preparatory Neptunian stage, we have the following indicators:

NEPTUNE	URANUS
rays two and six	rays one and seven
subjective realization	objective manifestation
understanding spirit	manifesting spirit
focussed love	focussed will

| psychological guide | dynamic leader |
| indicating need for change | effecting change |

D. K. give a comparison between these two planets:

"Neptune—Mystical consciousness or that innate sensitivity which leads unerringly to the higher vision, to the recognition of the inter-relation involved in man's essential duality during the process of manifestation, plus the activity of the mediator.
"Uranus—Occult consciousness or that intelligent, fusing condition which produces the scientific at-one-ment of the two factors, higher and lower self, through the intelligent use of the mind" (p. 306).

Neptune	Uranus
mystic	occult
sensitivity	intelligence
envisioning	manifesting
mediating	fusing higher and lower
duality	at-one-ment
unity	synthesis

The distinction that D. K. makes throughout His writings between the mystic and occultist is that the mystic tends to operate more along lines of feeling, sensitivity and heart, whereas the occultist works more mentally and scientifically, with a clear recognition of forms (both gross and subtle), energies and causes. The way of "divine knowledge" replaces the "mystic way of feeling" (Bailey, 1951, p. 224). The exoteric scientist studies the physical world scientifically. The occultist studies both the physical and subtle worlds scientifically.

Looking at it from the "vertical" angle with Neptune and Uranus as key energies that condition comprehensively the particular esoteric stage of development, Uranus or the spirit aspect is inclusive of the Neptunian sensitivity and consciousness aspect. In other words, the Uranus stage focusses on will-manifestation, but the initiate has already developed the love and mystic aspect—otherwise he/she would be shattered by the will. In our listing, then, the implied duality of love-will and subjective-objective, etc., is an erroneous one, since the higher is inclusive of the lower. The listing, however, is an aid in seeing the shift in focus rather than an exclusive polarity.

Soren Kierkegaard. As we ponder on D. K.'s outline and endeavor to discern the meaning and guard against personality distortion, it is often helpful (though difficult at this "very advanced stage") to find an illustrative example. Soren Kierkegaard (1813–1855) was a Danish philosopher and prolific writer whose life task had to do with nothing less than a "revision of Christianity. It is a matter of eliminating 1800 years as though they never had been. That I shall succeed therein I believe fully and firmly; all is clear as day to me. Yet I feel more and more acutely that at the least impatience, the least wilfulness, I am halted, my thoughts grow confused. I rise in the morning and thank God—and then I start my work. At a set hour in the evening I stop, and thank God—and then I go to sleep. And so I live, though not, at certain moments, without fits of melancholy and sadness, yet in the main, day in and day out in the most blissful enchantment" (Kierkegaard, p. 137). That Christianity needed revision, there is no doubt. The task was Herculean. When I read Kierkegaard, I have the feeling that no one understood Christ and Christianity (and also Socrates) until Kierkegaard. If one was truly to

revise Christianity, then one had to artfully destroy
the illusions that permeated the church and the so-
called "Christian" societies and nations. In Kierkegaard we find a highly developed love-wisdom quality,
a creative genius, and a selfless, sacrificial will that
powerfully effected change. Kierkegaard wrote in his
journal: "Suffering terrible inner torment I became a
writer. Then year after year I went on being a writer
and suffered for the sake of the Idea, in addition to
which I bore my inner sufferings. Then 1848 came.
That helped. There came a moment when, blissfully
overwhelmed, I dared to say to myself: I have compre-
hended the Highest. In truth, such a thing is not
vouchsafed to many in each generation. But almost in
the same instant something new came crashing down
on me: the Highest, after all, is not to *comprehend* the
Highest, but to do it.

"It is true that I had been aware of this from the
very start; that is why I am something else again than
an author in the ordinary sense of the word. On the
other hand, I did not realize so clearly that by having
private means and being independent it was easier for
me to express existentially the thing I had compre-
hended. Then when I understood *that,* I was willing to
stand forth as a writer, since having private means
made action easier for me than for other writers.

"But here it is again: the Highest is *not to comprehend* the Highest, but *to do it,* and note this well,
including all the burdens it involves. Only then did I
properly understand that 'Mercy' must find a place in
the plan; if not, a human being would suffocate the
moment he was about to start. But, but—'Mercy'
should not be included to prevent effort, so here it is

again: the Highest is not to comprehend the Highest, but to do it" (p. 146).

One might say that the comprehension of matters, that is to say, profound understanding, has to do with the consciousness-heart-soul aspect. But here we find an energy that demands or impels an immediate doing. This was a "blissful" alignment. D. K. has mentioned in connection with the three major stages the following progression of "happiness:"

personality . . . . .happiness
soul . . . . .joy
spirit, monad . . . . .bliss

Three times Kierkegaard repeats: "the Highest, after all, is not to comprehend the Highest, but to do it." Comprehension implies duality. But the comprehension (second aspect) of the Highest (the will or first aspect), resulting in doing (the third aspect) is not a duality but a synthesis. It is significant also that the helping of 1848 occurred when Kierkegaard was 35 years old. This is the will sub-cycle of the consciousness major cycle (see Abraham, 1984, pp. 68–75).

It is important, it seems to me, that Kierkegaard saw writing not as a self-chosen profession, with all the subtle little egotisms that career and profession imply. Rather it was God's will, or part of the doing that the Highest impelled. He describes his need to write in the following way: "So powerful an urge, so ample, so inexhaustible, one which, having subsisted day after day for five or six years, is still flowing as richly as ever, such an urge, one would think, must be a vocation from God. If these great riches of thought, still latent in my soul, must be repressed, it will be anguish and torture for me, and I shall become an ab-solute good-for-nothing. . . . It is hard and depressing to exhaust one's capital in order to be allowed to work more industriously and more strenuously than any man in the kingdom of Denmark. It is hard and de-pressing that as a result of all this toil one becomes the butt of the craven jealousy of the aristocracy and of the mockery of the populace! It is hard and depressing that the outlook is this: If I work still harder things will become still worse! . . . Being an author . . . is not self-chosen; it is concomitant with everything in my individuality and its deepest urge. . . . I must again sail the high seas, live willy-nilly, surrendering myself unconditionally to God's will. Of course it is more se-cure to have a solid position in life, some official ap-pointment which does not demand nearly as much of one—but in God's name, the other thing, by God, is still more secure. But it takes faith; you need faith at every turn, every instant. That is the difference. Most people lead far too sheltered lives, and for that reason they get to know God so little. They have permanent positions, they never put in their utmost effort; they have tranquility with wife and children—and I, for one, shall never talk deprecatingly about that happiness—but I believe it is my task to do without all this. Why in the world should that which we read in the New Testa-ment again and again not be permitted? But the unfor-tunate thing is that people have no idea at all of what it means to be a Christian, and that is why I am left without sympathy, that is why I am not understood" (Kierkegaard, pp. 52, 53, 54).

Elsewhere in his diary Kierkegaard writes: "I served Thought and Truth in such a way as not to derive any secular and temporal advantages therefrom. . . As my work progressed I constantly thought that I was gaining a better understanding of God's will with me, that I bear the anguish whereby God has put his reins on me" (p. 58).

In the previous Neptunian stage of soul unfoldment the aspirant and disciple dealt with problems of attuning to the vision, developing the heart or love-wisdom nature, of sensitivity to the subtle, invisible worlds, etc. With all these qualities already developed, we see Kierkegaard laboring primarily to better "understand God's will with me." Some of the results or conditions that accompany such a labor are:

1) An alignment with the Highest that immediately demands a *doing*.

2) Great riches of thought and an inexhaustible flow of ideas.

3) Strenuous labor, the right use of time, giving the utmost effort.

4) Not a self-chosen profession that seeks personal security and personal aggrandizement, but following a God-chosen path with all the day-to-day risk and rejection that that implies.

5) Another condition has to do with placing Truth at the highest, or serving Truth primarily. Or as Kierkegaard writes elsewhere, purity of heart is to *will one thing* and that is to *will the good*. Willing one thing may mean the same as "having no other Gods before one." This is a very rare state of mind. The usual condition Kierkegaard refers to as "doublemindedness." There are areas or subtle attitudes in our lives that we are not yet ready to open up to the eradicating will of God.

"Every human being," according to Kierkegaard, "is born with the seed of primitivity, for primitivity means a possibility for developing the spirit." Intellectual and worldly knowledge tends to destroy one's primitivity. "Christianity has relation to developing one's primitivity. Destroy your primitivity, and you will probably get along well in the world, maybe achieve great success—but Eternity will reject you. Follow your primitivity, and you will be shipwrecked in temporality, but accepted by Eternity" (p. 159).

Primitivity here is related to spirit, to being, to life. No matter where we are in terms of level, the spirit (or our inner most being) is there to indicate the next step ahead. "Primitivity" calls our attention to its opposite or the tendency of "civilized" intellectual man to step out of the flow in his illusory and glamorous personal quests and temporarily to lose the connective thread with spirit. Primitivity also calls our attention to the will in that it implies a livingness, a doing, and a synthesis with the natural forces. The implication is that there is an energy-quality here that needs to be maintained, rather than lost as one develops knowledge. In this regard we find another interesting statement: "Most people," writes Kierkegaard, "live devoid of ideas; then there are the very few who relate themselves poetically to the ideal, but refute it in their personal lives. In that way parsons are poets, and being parsons they are, in a much deeper sense than poets, 'deceivers,' as Socrates already called the poets. . . . Priests, professors of philosophy and poets now occupy the position as servants of the Truth—which I imagine is quite advantageous to them—though less so to Truth" (p. 65).

Once again, is not Kierkegaard drawing our attention to some aspect of the will? To live devoid of ideas is to lack any *depth of consciousness and reflection* beyond the immediate personal survival and gratification. But to be consciously aware and not to live it, is lack of will. The Sun in this sense, veils Uranus— the vitalization, manifestation and dynamic vivification of the idea.

"Believing that his sins have been forgiven," writes Kierkegaard, "is the decisive crisis through which a human being becomes spirit." Kierkegaard sees the lower aspect of man (what we would call personality) as sinful. This aspect has a "corrupting effect as soon as it gets the least bit of leeway." This is identical with Blavatsky's statement that lower man is moved by "selfishness and egotism in every instance." Kierkegaard identifies sinning as either *specific* or *general.* The childlike notion is that we commit a *specific* sin, then ask forgiveness for it. The asssumption is that we are good and occasionally commit a sin. This, however, perpetuates the sinning and, therefore, leaves man unchanged. Sinning not in the specific but in the *general* sense has to do with the realization that as self-centered personalities, our general nature is one of sinning and one of having a corrupting influence. To realize this profoundly is then to struggle not with an occasional sin but with the whole lower nature. This then sets up a relationship with the spirit, which demands a continuous willing to be a spirit, to be good. Here we have the possibility of realizing that our sinning in thought, feeling and action has been divinely forgiven—and then profound change is probable. At this point "all selfish clinging to the world and to its own self [personality], is lost. Now, humanly speaking, he is old, extremely old, but from the viewpoint of eternity he is young" (pp. 153–154).

"Christianity is right: sin is guilt," Kierkegaard remarks. "For when a man does not do right, it is quite rightly because he does not understand it; if he understood it, etc. But the reason he does not under-stand what is right is that he cannot understand it, and that he cannot understand it is because he *will* not understand it—so there is the rub" (p. 126).

Transition From Neptune to Uranus. In Alice Bailey's book *Discipleship in the New Age* the Master D. K. gives personal instructions to a group of disciples. The disciple D. A. O. has a seventh ray soul and a first ray personality. This disciple's struggle may shed some light on the transition from "Neptune" to "Uranus."

D. K. informs D. A. O. that "the sense of the abstract and the formless was unduly developed in you. You were the true mystic and the spiritual visionary, the idealist and the one whose imagination, love of beauty and the sense of inner reality shut you away from practical life. . . . The blending, merging and fusing of the subjective beauty and the outer beautiful reality is your daily task. Those who, like you, are intuitives, must train themselves to be interpreters. The task of the interpreter of reality and of beauty should increasingly drive you into organized and planned activity" (Bailey, 1944, p. 287).

"Aim at real achievement in accomplishment. . . . These achievements (of a minor character and of a major character) must be tangible, and should be the emergence into being of that which can be realized as the externalization of your inner subjective perceptions. Intuitives (such as you are) have ever the problem of their materializing" (p. 285).

We have then Neptune development:

—sense of abstract and formless
—mystic, spiritual visionary

—idealist
—love of beauty
—intuitive
—imaginative

And the subsequent need for the development of the energy of Uranus:

—blend inner with outer beauty
—interpret (the inner to the outer)
—organized and planned activity
—tangible achievements
—externalize subjective perceptions
—materialization

D. K. points out to D. A. O. that the limitation of the mystic is the tendency to "find one's peace and relaxation in a well-intended spiritual withdrawing and isolation." There is a need, however, to realize that the "physical plane in the chosen field of expression is *spiritual achievement*" (p. 268).

The *wholistic* factors here deal with:

1. Recognizing an overdeveloped quality and working to develop its *balancing opposite*. (Mystic Neptune developed, Uranus needed to spiritualize physical plane living).
2. Recognizing a *latent* quality that needs developing (a seventh ray soul).
3. Recognizing the *cycle* or appropriate *time* to go on to other work.

Strictly speaking, D. A. O. might have been a disciple and not an initiate in the technical sense of those terms, and therefore not a true example of the energy of Uranus at the spirit-will level. Nevertheless, the

Master's words to D. A. O. do shed much light on the transition from mystic to practical occultist or white magician, which archetypally speaks to the Neptune-Uranus transition. It is necessary to keep in mind that something of these energies play upon a person both "horizontally" and "vertically." We could represent the three major levels under discussion and the three energies in the following manner:

```
Spirit-Will ................Vulcan, Neptune, URANUS
Soul-Consciousness..........Vulcan, NEPTUNE, Uranus
Personality Form ...........VULCAN, Neptune, Uranus
```

Each level wholistically includes all three. At each level there is a special emphasis on one, where the energy "rules" in a special way. The lower energy is only a dim, distorted version of the higher. The higher includes or synthesizes the lower. It is a mistake to think of the soul in a purely Neptunian, mystical way, for the soul certainly includes much practical service and dynamic, outer spiritual livingness. Yet the soul is the Heart aspect, the consciousness aspect, so esoteric Neptune plays a major role in the full flowering of the love and wisdom nature. One might also add that it is a mistake to think of *esoteric* Uranus in simply organizational terms, since it is so imbued with will.

The Esoteric Influence. As another indication of the various levels on which a planet can have an influence, consider the following passage from *Esoteric Astrology:* "No planet falls in Leo and no planet is exalted in this sign, whilst the power of both Uranus and Saturn is somewhat lessened, *except in the case of* *the initiate who responds powerfully to the esoteric influence of Uranus* (p. 310. my italics). How can we appreciate the relatively exalted consciousness of an initiate? How can we see the "higher octaves" of planetary energy? How can we avoid the tendency to assign to the higher what we are experiencing on a lower level? Some indications of Uranus controlling on a high level are that the person becomes "the true observer, detached from the material side of life, but utilizing it as he pleases. His spiritual consciousness is capable of a great expression and he can be both an electric, dynamic leader, a pioneer in new fields of endeavor and also a magnetic center of a group. . . . He is then polarized above the diaphragm, for the lower material aspects of life have really no great appeal to him" (Bailey, 1951, p. 309). The seventh ray Uranian energy controls the seventh or etheric-physical plane. This means organizational energies-abilities, since organization (as well as will) is a key factor in controlling the physical. Organization has to do with knowing how things are accomplished, that is, how a system functions, the hierarchical order, needs and demands, what simplifies and synthesizes, what motivates, what is possible at the present time, the timing, the cycle, the governing principle, knowing where the energy is blocked and how it circulates. At the personality level there is a tendency to use the Uranian energy in a personal way. The personality, however, comes to realize the shallowness, the hollowness of its personal power and success. Uranus at the initiate level is "detached from the material side, but utilizes it as he pleases." Detachment from the material side would include detachment from the physical, emotional and mental worlds—the worlds of personality

involvement. The initiate has "killed out all longing
for the forms of those planes" (Bailey, *Light of the
Soul,* p. 138). The form side can be utilized by the initiate but for what purposes? One could probably say for
the helping of humanity to gain detachment from
form and working knowledge of the spirit (moving
from mother nurturing to father laboring). Form can
be spiritually utilized, when it is not misused for fearful, covetous, self-aggrandizing purposes. Then the
form becomes radiant. Then the form is aligned with
spirit. Then the form is not tainted and defiled and
polluted by personal desires. The task of Uranus and
the initiate is to restore form to its spiritual purposes.
In a certain sense one could say, the disciple awakens
consciousness and the initiate revitalizes the energy
body, the etheric form.

The initiate's task is far more difficult, due to
personality's tenacious grip on the form aspect. In
other words, a certain degree of consciousness raising
is tolerated, but the battle becomes intensified when
the "keys to the city" or the organization, the power
unit, changes hands. But once again let us remind
ourselves that the pattern can be found on all levels,
and that disciples work with form as well as consciousness. Yet the initiate's use of the will alters form more
immediately, more unequivocally. The great initiate
and Master Jesus, the Avatar, had no possessions, no
title, no property. He had the power to heal, to love,
and to teach about the Kingdom of Heaven. He was a
greater threat to the established religious order than
he was to the political order, and it was the former
that conspired against Him. The energy that He an-
chored etherically on earth conditioned the subsequent 2000 years.

APPENDIX

Constellations and Planetary Rulers
In Connection with Ordinary Man

Constellation	Ruler	Ray
1. Aries	Mars	6th ray
2. Taurus	Venus	5th ray
3. Gemini	Mercury	4th ray
4. Cancer	Moon	4th ray
5. Leo	The Sun	2nd ray
6. Virgo	Mercury	4th ray
7. Libra	Venus	5th ray
8. Scorpio	Mars	6th ray
9. Sagittarius	Jupiter	2nd ray
10. Capricorn	Saturn	3rd ray
11. Aquarius	Uranus	7th ray
12. Pisces	Jupiter	2nd ray

Constellations and Planetary Rulers
In Connection with Disciples and Initiates

Constellation	Ruler	Ray
1. Aries	Mercury	4th ray
2. Taurus	Vulcan	1st ray
3. Gemini	Venus	5th ray
4. Cancer	Neptune	6th ray
5. Leo	The Sun veiling a hidden planet (Neptune 6th ray)	
6. Virgo	The Moon veiling a hidden planet (Vulcan, 1st ray)	
7. Libra	Uranus	7th ray
8. Scorpio	Mars	6th ray
9. Sagittarius	The Earth	3rd ray
10. Capricorn	Saturn	3rd ray
11. Aquarius	Jupiter	2nd ray
12. Pisces	Pluto	1st ray

(Bailey, *Esoteric Astrology*, p. 66.)

Bibliography

Abraham, Kurt. *Psychological Types and the Seven Ray, vol. I.* New Jersey: Lampus Press, 1983.
———*Threefold Method for Understanding the Seven Rays and Other Essays in Esoteric Psychology.* New Jersey: Lampus Press, 1984.
Addams, Jane. *Twenty Years at Hull-House with Autobiographical Notes.* New York: MacMillian, 1928.
Bailey, Alice A. *Discipleship in the New Age, vol. I.* New York: Lucis Publishing Co., 1944.
———*Esoteric Astrology.* New York: Lucis Publishing Co., 1951.
———*Esoteric Healing.* New York: Lucis Publishing Co., 1953.
———*Glamour: A World Problem.* New York: Lucis Publishing Co., 1950.
———*Light of the Soul.* New York: Lucis Publishing Co., 1955.
———*Rays and Initiations.* New York: Lucis Publishing Co., 1960.
———*Treatise on Cosmic Fire.* New York: Lucis Publishing Co., 1925.
———*Treatise on White Magic.* New York: Lucis Publishing Co., 1934.
Blavatsky, H. P. *Isis Unveiled, A Master-Key to the Mysteries of Ancient and Modern Science and Theology.* Pasadena, CA: Theosophical University Press, 1960.
———*The Secret Doctrine.* Adyar, India: The Theosophical Publishing House, 1938.
Ferguson, Marylyn. "Karl Pribram's Changing Real-

ity" in *The Holographic Paradigm and other Paradoxes*, edited by Ken Wilber. Boston: New Science Library, Shambhala, 1982.

Fromm, Erich. "The Nature of Well-Being" in *The Awakening Heart*, edited by John Welwood. Boston: New Science Library, Shambhala Publications, 1983.

Graves, Robert. *The Greek Myths*. New York: George Braziller, Inc., 1955.

Heart. New York: Agni Yoga Society, 1932.

James, William. *The Varieties of Religious Experience*. New York: MacMillian Publishing Co., 1961.

Kierkegaard, Soren. *The Diary of Soren Kierkegaard*, edited by Peter P. Rohde, translated by Gerda M. Andersen. New York: Philosophical Library, 1960.

Krishnamacharya, E. *Spiritual Astrology*. Visakhapatnam, India: 1966.

Leo, Alan. *Art of Synthesis*. London: L. N. Fowler & Co., 1968.

Norelli-Bachelet, Patrizia. *The Gnostic Circle*. Panorama City, CA: Aeon Books, 1975.

Norris, A. G. S. *Transcendental Astrology*. New York: Samuel Weiser, 1974.

Plato. *Great Dialogues of Plato*, edited by W. H. D. Rouse and Eric Warmington, translated by W. H. D. Rouse. New York: New American Library, 1956.

Storm, Hyemeyohsts. *Seven Arrows*. New York: Random House, 1972.

Walsh, Roger. "Things Are Not As They Seem" in *The Awakening Heart*, ed. John Welwood. Boston: New Science Library, Shambhala Publications, 1983.

Wilber, Ken. *Up From Eden, A Transpersonal View of Human Evolution*. Boston: New Science Library, Shambhala Publications, 1986.

INDEX